QUEST FOR THE
LOST WORLD

QUEST FOR THE LOST WORLD

BRIAN BLESSED

BOXTREE

First published 1999 by Boxtree an imprint of Macmillan Publishers Ltd
25 Eccleston Place London SW1W 9NF
Basingstoke and Oxford

www.macmillan.co.uk

Associated companies throughout the world

ISBN 0 7522 1752 6

1 3 5 7 9 8 6 4 2

A CIP catalogue record for this book
is available from the British Library.

Typeset by SX Composing DTP, Rayleigh, Essex

Printed by The Bath Press, Bath

This book is dedicated to
Explore Worldwide
and Anthony Rivas Merrill

CONTENTS

ACKNOWLEDGEMENTS

Writing this book has proved to be a delightful experience. Rekindling wonderful memories of people, places and events from my adventures and escapades has been all the more enjoyable for giving me the opportunity to work with people I admire and love. The book has been a tremendous team effort. For entrusting treasured photographs I owe an immense debt of gratitude to Explore Worldwide, Suzi Poole, Cedric Webster, Nick and Marianne Moss, Rosalind Blessed, Steve Bell of Himalayan Kingdoms, D.C. Thompson, the Natural History Photographic Agency and Lucas films for the photograph of Boss Nass from the film *Star Wars I: The Phantom Menace*. Hearty thanks must go to Gilbert C. Higson, who conveyed to me with appropriate drama the story of Barnburgh's 'Cat and Man' church. My theatrical and literary agent, Derek Webster, has not spared himself running thither and yon on my behalf, using diplomacy, encouragement and love in dealing with this project. Derek is a truly remarkable man. I also owe his wonderful assistant Caz Swinfield many big hugs and kisses for her hard work and kindness. I am similarly grateful to Boxtree, my admirable new publishers, not least for bringing me into contact with the talented Senior Commissioning Editor, Jenny Olivier, who has delighted me with her vivid imagination, scholarship and vision. Also many thanks to Lee Bekker, Senior Production Controller, for her wonderful creative work, Sarah Bennie, Publicity Director, for her inspirational planning, Clare Hulton, Editorial Director, for her wisdom and kindness, and Adrian Sington, Managing Director, for his inspired leadership.

My P.A. Stephen Gittins worked heroically on every aspect of the book, a minor miracle when you consider he has been managing the ponies and horses and every furry and feathered creature around my home, as well as organizing my professional life. I am also grateful to Adrian Rigelsford for introducing me to Boxtree.

Whenever I became bogged down and uncertain, my wife Hildegard lent a sympathetic ear and guided me in a new direction. Her amused tolerance of my appalling spelling amazed me as, with love, dedication, and a keen professional eye, she encouraged and stimulated me until the book finally took shape. Without her inspiration it would never have been written.

'South America is a place I love, and I think if you take it right through from Darien to Fuego, it's the grandest, richest, most wonderful bit of earth upon this planet.

'Now, down here in the Matto Grosso,' he swept his cigar over a part of the map, 'or up in this corner where three countries meet, nothin' would surprise me. As Professor Challenger said tonight, there are 50,000 miles of waterway running through a forest that is very near the size of Europe. Why shouldn't somethin' new and wonderful lie in such a country? And why shouldn't we be the men to find it out?'

Sir Arthur Conan Doyle, *The Lost World*

PROLOGUE

This book is about fulfilling a childhood dream. A dream of reaching and exploring the mysterious primeval plateau of Mount Roraima, the fabled 'Lost World', immortalized by Sir Arthur Conan Doyle in his book of the same name.

I worship nature! Throughout my life I have also constantly burned with an insatiable craving for adventure, for knowledge and for new experiences – probing the unknown for new mental and physical thresholds. Oh! Adventure! Adventure! Dear God in Heaven! Give me adventure unlimited and my oh my, what a wonderful blue orb we live on.

To see our Mother Earth on film from space fills me with sweet hope and boundless optimism. Come, my gallant reader, join hands with me and embark on a quest that as the Ghost in *Hamlet* says will,

> *Make thy two eyes, like stars, start from their spheres;*
> *Thy knotted and combined locks to part,*
> *And each particular hair to stand on end,*
> *Like quills, upon the fretful porpentine.*
>
> Act I, Scene v

At 17.00 hours on 18 July 1998, I placed my head on my rucksack, stretched out my 16.5 stones (114 kg) on a sturdy wooden bench in the weeny airport of Canaima in deepest Venezuela and took in my exotic surroundings.

A short distance away I could see the banks of a beautiful lagoon with the Salto Hacha (Hacha Falls) on the far side and several *tepuis* (mountains) forming a staggering backdrop. The tropical afternoon sun shone gloriously, and periodically a red, black and yellow 'postman' (*Heliconius melpomene*) butterfly would flutter by. Peace and perfect bliss inside and out.

I had been part of a small expedition, led by guide Anthony Rivas, which included three women and seven men and a dozen or so Pemon and Kamaracoto Indians. It meant that I had just completed the first phase of that childhood dream of mine, to explore the Lost World of the Gran Sabana (Great Savanna) in the south-east of Venezuela. I intended to return later in the year to complete my quest but what a happy expedition this had been. Apart from me (aged 62) everyone on the expedition was from the jolly ranks of youth! Nevertheless, they had accepted me with great generosity of spirit.

They were a lively bunch of lads and lasses from all walks of life, and it had been a privilege to explore with such rare spirits. Together we had ascended ancient mountains, sweated through tropical rain forests, swooned at dense clouds of electric blue morpho butterflies, marvelled at dawns of delight, canoed and swum into the bowels of giant canyons. Now, sadly, it was time to say goodbye. But where was our plane? It was hours late.

During the afternoon numerous twin-engined light aircraft had landed on the dusty airstrip and, after unloading their passengers, mainly gold miners going on vacation, had quickly loaded up more people from other expeditions and sped on their way, leaving us feeling strangely deserted and lonely. We joked about it but we were becoming increasingly concerned. Time was passing by and the once bright sun was now taking on a golden hue as it journeyed towards the distant horizon. A strange silence pervaded the little airport. Finally it was broken by the distant sound of an old Dakota approaching from the direction of Canaima Lagoon. We all felt relieved and ran out to greet the incoming plane.

As its quaint engines stopped, we gathered around it like a troop of baboons and loudly enquired if it was our flight. We received a rather brusque 'no' from the two unsmiling pilots and returned sheepishly to the shade of the rustic lounge.

Fifteen minutes later the Dakota took off and also disappeared into the wide blue yonder and the airstrip once again fell into an uneasy silence.

It was important for us to reach Aeropuerto Caracas by nightfall as we had been informed that it would close once it was dark. In the event of that happening we would be diverted to some obscure airport many miles outside the city. We simply had to get back to Caracas so that on the following morning we could catch our scheduled flight back to London. Underneath it all, I personally didn't give a damn, I would have been quite happy to canoe back to Caracas.

And then, just as we were about to give it up as a bad job, miracle of miracles, another plane hovered over the distant *tepuis* and powered its way towards us across the lagoon.

'This has to be it,' our guide Anthony cried.

I immediately burst into some obscure song from my past, ' "*Then out of an orange-coloured sky, wham, bam, alakazam, wonderful you came by!*" '

This plane was a small 25-seater Let 410, type YVC5985, made in Czechoslovakia. It had two propellers and looked new and sturdy. Forming a straight line, we humbly and tentatively enquired if the plane was for the British contingent. 'Yes,' growled the bad-tempered Captain (whose name was Ismail Urdaneta), 'hurry up or we miss the light!'

He really was in a stinking mood. On approaching the aircraft we had noticed that he and his younger co-pilot were having a hell of a row, God knows about what, but their behaviour didn't fill us with confidence. They were quite obviously mortified at being late. 'Three hours,' they shouted, 'three hours and it will be dark.'

We didn't have to be told twice. Like well-drilled soldiers we formed a human chain and powered our luggage into the cabin at a rate of knots. The Brits then boarded 'toot sweet' leaving the two pilots gaping. Twenty-two days of bold endeavour had left us in great shape.

Inside the cabin I slapped the middle-aged pilot on the back and saluted him as Captain Nemo. In the same breath I burst into another daft song – ' "*Oh you can fly, fly, fly stormy water, oh you can take me to the bottom of the sea.*" '

This alarmed the Captain and he slowly backed down the small gangway to his seat muttering nervously 'Tie seat-belts, tie seat-belts pronto.'

Come to think of it, I did look rather wild and woolly at that moment. My unkempt beard covered most of my face and my appearance was not dissimilar to the description of the King of the Apemen in Doyle's *Lost World*. Obviously having the missing link on board his plane was an unnerving experience. I therefore suppressed my atavistic nature and became a 'good yeti' and strapped myself into my seat.

The plane took off with a roar and we were homeward bound. There was an air of celebration on board as Anthony conjured up a tuck box secreted at the back of the plane. What a charming host he had been! Tall, slim, dark and handsome, he had catered for our every need. Between handing out sandwiches and cans of drink he once more waxed lyrical about his beloved Venezuela.

I had filmed the expedition on a digital video camera, a very impressive piece of machinery. Poor camera! I had subjected it to all the rigours of the primeval wilderness of the Gran Sabana. Inside the instruction book was written the words 'Do not expose this camera to rain or moisture.' Rain or moisture – I ask you. How can you possibly avoid it in Venezuela?

My camera had been exposed to steaming rain forests, rampaging rivers, gigantic waterfalls and tropical storms and, to my utter amazement it had come through it all without a scratch! Still fully operational.

I focused its eager lens on Anthony's glowing features. 'Oh no!' he protested smilingly, 'not more filming. Spare me – Professor Challenger.'

It was a fair comparison, as I was of similar build to the character in Conan Doyle's novel, and sported the same large beard.

'Come on Anthony,' I shouted. 'You cannot avoid your destiny. This film is going to make you the biggest star in the western hemisphere. Now tell us the history of the Gran Sabana and the Lost World.'

There was no response from the young man and he tried to avert his gaze, but I wouldn't let him off the hook. 'Come on Anthony, I've charged up these batteries at tremendous expense. Come on – tell me a story before I go to bed.'

Wiping his brow and smiling shyly but proudly the poor lad began his tale.

'Venezuela's most haunting and astonishing terrain is the Gran Sabana, a valley of more than one hundred 'flat-topped' mountains, their sheer walls the ultimate test for climbers, their tops covered with prehistoric sandstone, labyrinths and dense foliage. The Gran Sabana, 3,300 feet [990 m] above sea level is home to the Roraima Tepui, reaching 9,220 feet [2,810 m] above sea level.'

Yes, Roraima, the Lost World, really exists.

'Situated in the extreme south-east of Venezuela, at the junction with Brazil and Guyana, Roraima is an extraordinary mountain with vertical walls. It soars above the surrounding savannah and tropical forest like some vast, impregnable fortress. About 85 per cent of Roraima's area belongs to Venezuela, 10 per cent to Guyana and 5 per cent to Brazil.

'The *tepuis* are remote and scattered over an area of some 200,000 square miles (500,000 sq km). Many of them are concealed by dense cloud cover, like the surface of some distant planet. Only a fraction of Roraima's 44 square miles (115 sq km) has so far been explored.'

At this point in the story Anthony paused for refreshment, but, after a good swig of fizzy orange, he continued his yarn.

'Until recently no one knew Roraima's age. Then a few years ago geologists found places where molten rock had thrust its way between layers of sandstone after the ancient plateaus were formed. They conducted chronological dating tests on the igneous diabase and other rocks and came up with an outstanding result: the sandstone was at least 1.8 billion years old. Which means that Roraima dates back to a period before even the most primitive life forms existed in the oceans. It would be another 1.2 billion years before plants and animals emerged from these oceans to live on land.

'Roraima's sedimentary rock was already old-aged when South America and Africa were joined together in the prehistoric continent known as Gondwana. Gondwana had, of course, been part of the initial gigantic continent named Pangea. Gondwana itself began to break up some 135 million years ago, yet evidence of the original junction still exists: cliffs and mesa-like mountains in the Western Sahara consist of sandstone similar to that of Mount Roraima.'

Anthony stopped at this point and I thought his short history lesson was over. Not so, once more he replenished himself with a liberal gulp of juice and then carried on his merry way.

His gift for storytelling, combined with his love for the subject matter, made him irresistible. Speaking quietly he now took us into the realms of mystery and legend.

'In Pemon Indian mythology, Roraima's summit is the territory over which Kuin reigns. She is the goddess who gives *Kachira* (casava-based liquor) to her visitors, as well as the music of the *tepui*'s winds as welcome gifts. According to the Pemon Indians, the correct name of Mount Roraima is *Roroima*. The word *Roroi* means 'bluish-green' and *ma* means 'big': The Big Bluish-green Mountain. The Pemones Arekunas called it *Loloima*, and it sounds like 'Dodoima' in the Yekuana and Makiritare languages. One Makiritare legend relates that the mountain is the remains of a giant sacred tree, felled by mythical animals in order to create the yucca and all other fruit of the Earth obtained by man.'

Chuckling away like a naughty little boy, Anthony continued, 'If all that sounds strange and confusing, allow me to confuse you even more, Professor Challenger. Roraima really is an extraordinary mountain, and is aptly called the Mother of All Waters. Three rivers have their source on its summit. The Arabopo river starts in the vast Venezuelan sector and pours into the Kukenan which, in turn, flows into the Caroni and, from there, into the Orinoco river. The Kako river originates in Guyana's sector. This river flows into the Mazzaruni, which pours into the Essequibo river. The waters of the Cotingo river originate in Brazil's sector and they flow into the Branco river, which pours into the Rio Negro, the waters of which finally go into the Amazonas.'

'That's a lot of water, Anthony,' I laughed.

'Yes, indeed a lot of water, Challenger,' he replied. 'Do you want me to go on?'

'Just a little,' I responded. 'I've got about five minutes left on my tape. I want to save some of it. Could you give me two minutes on Alexander Laime's dinosaurs? Hold on, I want to get in closer on your face. And what a handsome face it is too. Eat your heart out Leonardo DiCaprio!

'Alexander Laime was a keen, well-respected student of wildlife on the *tepuis*. For many years he lived alone in the wilderness on a small island in the Carrao, about a day's journey by canoe on the Carrao river from Canaima. Alexander cleared an area of jungle on his island for a garden, where he grew bananas, manioc, potatoes, pumpkins and mangoes. He lived in a palm-thatched wooden hut that he built himself. Beside the door hung a 'Plumb Bob' on a string by which he kept track of the damage from termites, which continually devoured his hut.

'In 1955 he made an expedition to Auyan Tepui [Devil's Mountain], whose summit stretches over a 270-square-mile [700 sq km] area, and which, as well as being the biggest *tepui* in the Lost World, is also famed for the Angel Falls, which leap from its northern face, and for another ten or twenty waterfalls, all among the highest in the world. He claimed that on this expedition, whilst searching for diamonds in one of the rivers on top of Auyan Tepui, he encountered three 'dinosaur-like lizards'. He said they were sunbathing on a rocky ledge above the river. At first he thought they were seals, but when he sneaked closer, he saw that they were creatures with enormously long necks and ageless reptilian faces. Each had four 'scale-covered' fins instead of legs.

'Laime made some drawings of the creatures – they resembled plesiosaurs, marine reptiles that became extinct 65 million years ago. Some scientists think that he saw a large species of tropical otter that has a long neck, but the local Indians point out that rivers on Auyan Tepui are not known to contain fish, the otter's principal food, and thus it is unlikely that otters would exist there.

'I'm afraid the scientific world did not take his claims seriously. Many people considered him a bit crazy. The wild man who lived alone at the base of Auyan Tepui and communed with dinosaurs. His standing as a student of wildlife fell considerably. He died a short while ago, otherwise we could have met and discussed the sighting with him. By all accounts he was a kind and affable man.'

'How did *you* feel about him, Anthony?' I injected.

'Oh I have an open mind about the whole affair. Laime was a serious, meticulous man. In this part of the world new species of animals and plants are discovered all the time. I think it would be wrong to write off his claim. Maybe you and I can get together, Professor Challenger, and explore that remote part of the Auyan Tepui where he saw the plesiosaurs. Are you game for that?'

'Just tell me when,' I replied.

We shook hands on the matter.

'You must understand,' continued Anthony, '60 per cent of the *tepuis* have not been explored, and most of the others have only been visited fleetingly. Take Roraima itself. Its great Northern Labyrinth is completely unexplored. It's a terrifying place! The Kamaracoto Indians say there are diamonds to be found in the Labyrinth, but they steadfastly refuse to set foot in there! Unearthly screams emanate from it. Expeditions that have tried to make a thorough exploitation of the region have perished there. The last to die were a group of Germans. It's a 3-mile [5 km] region of jumbled rock towers and dark, slimy deep chasms, some as deep as Roraima is high! During violent thunderstorms some of these monstrous chasms rapidly fill with raging water and drown any occupants. It goes without saying that the area is teeming with scorpions and poisonous spiders. You really need the luck of the devil if you are going to survive in that place.

'Take Auyan Tepui, north-west of Roraima, which we have been flying over – its size is incomprehensible!'

Anthony was really getting worked up now. A fine example, which we all shared, of '*tepui* fever'.

'Auyan Tepui is bordered by dense impenetrable tropical forests. Not every type of *tepui* has the same vegetation and there is no chance of a natural exchange among them. Each species of plant has adapted to its particular environment. This is because of millions of years of isolation. You ask me if Alexander Laime saw dinosaurs? Anything is possible in this land. I can tell you this – we have not begun to discover the secrets of the Gran Sabana.'

As Anthony concluded, I stood up, shook his hand, tweaked his nose and whispered, 'You are a star! A shining star in the firmament – thank you.'

I sat down and turned my attention to the stunning scenery below.

Various *tepuis* rose out of the vibrant green landscape like medieval castles.

Some of these formidable structures were shrouded by clouds that changed shape and colour as they were suffused with the intense rays of the sun.

In a beautiful valley formed by the Acanan river, I could see two large, low *tepuis* covered in lush green vegetation. On the other side of the valley rose the walls of Auyan Tepui like a gigantic rock curtain across the whole horizon from north to south. Rivers with names like Mazaruni, Kako, Escquibo, Rupunini, and Churun stretched out as far as the eye could see. Directly to the south of the Auyan Tepui massif isolated peaks could be seen, silhouetted against the cobalt blue of the sky. My eyes peered downwards, trying to penetrate and solve the mysteries of the emerald forest. Unexplored green, green mansions of unknown delights.

The rapid journey of the afternoon sun, in company with the gradual build-up of altocumulus clouds, created sudden darts of light that revealed a plethora of shades of vegetation in half-hidden glades. Yet, the rain and cloud forests possessively hid its secrets from my gaze. Within its rampant growth, I knew there were gentle, slender tendrils that supported passion flowers of brilliant blue, deep crimson and rich ochreous yellow. In the overwhelming push for light were spider flowers, 500 different kinds of orchid, rampant ivies, tree ferns, podo carp trees, bamboos, bromeliads, orange calceolaria flowers, and worts with slipper-like pouches dancing in the humid breeze.

Throbbing with life, the dense canopy of trees contained bright red macaws, blue hummingbirds, butterflies, blue tree-frogs, silky anteaters, spider monkeys, water-loving tapirs, howler monkeys, capybaras, peccaries, ocelots, margays, jaguars, bush-master snakes, anacondas, and stinging ants emerging from cecropias trees to do battle with any insect that dare rival them.

The spectrum of wildlife in that luxuriant landscape was limitless. There was a haunting, dreamlike quality about this world. Yes, the jungle hides all. Millions of creatures in Venezuela zealously camouflage themselves from our gaze.

As I pressed my face against the window of the plane to take in another tantalizing piece of scenery, my eyes focused on several tracts of bare land, which bore evidence of man's greedy intrusion into this Garden of Eden: open-cast gold mines.

Although Venezuela is teeming with life, the rain forest ecosystem is very delicate. If the land is cleared for large-scale farming or gold mining, the shallow nutrients are leached out and washed away by the rains leaving a desert-like landscape. Miners leave behind rivers contaminated with mercury and holes that fill with rainwater to become breeding grounds for mosquitos. Venezuela has not suffered the same sort of environmental catastrophe as its neighbour Brazil, but the situation is volatile. The region has some legal protection. Let us hope it stays that way.

Besides three National Parks – Yacapana, Serrania De La Neblina and Duida-Marahuaca – certain areas are off limits to mining and tourism. Among these are the vast homelands of the primitive Yanomami Indians.

An hour later, my nose was once more pressed against the window as I caught sight of the great Orinoco river. Looking down from a height of 12,000 feet (3,650 m) the sun's rays made it look like a gigantic silver anaconda. This mighty river exhibits a rare phenomenon. During certain times of the year, instead of receiving waters from the smaller Rio Casiquiare, it reverses the flow and feeds part of its own volume into this inferior channel.

The Casiquiare then flows in the opposite direction from the Orinoco's main course, empties into the Rio Negro and flows on into the Amazon. This amazing phenomenon intrigues engineers even today.

On the Orinoco's banks the canopy of the rain forest is so thick and dense, it seems impenetrable. The forest contains 680 species of bird, including magnificently coloured toucans, parrots and multicoloured hummingbirds.

This paradise, of course, has its darker side. Beware all travellers who treat mosquitos lightly. On the Orinoco they attack from all sides and are merciless. Employ all the protection you can. The dreaded *el sudar y las moscas* ('the sweat and the flies') was an expression used first by the early Spanish explorers. With faces punctured by mosquito bites and blood running down their faces and arms they desperately sought the protection of the bark of the Cinchona tree, which provided Quinine – the earliest remedy for malaria. When the Spanish first took it back to Europe they renamed it 'Jesuits' Bark'.

To continue in this rather macabre vein, I must tell you that the rain forest floor abounds with scorpions, tarantulas and deadly fer-de-lance snakes, whilst the Orinoco harbours electric eels, piranhas, alligators, crocodiles and wandering bull sharks. On a lighter note it also contains delightful Arrau tortoises, pink fun-loving freshwater dolphins and carefree cow-sized manatees. All of these gorgeous 'beasties' are well-known and catalogued. Most reassuring.

But you never quite know what lurks in the murky Amazonian rivers. The natives speak in hushed tones of a grotesque giant snake, called the Cobra Grande, over 65 feet (20 m) long and 3 feet (1 m) in diameter, that has phosphorescent green eyes and horns on its head like the roots of a tree. On, on, it glides down the green Orinoco, through the darker Rio Casquiare, to the black waters of the Rio Negro. Once there, it finds a suitable dark, deep inlet and quietly celebrates by rhythmically rolling over and over again in primitive delight. At the climax of its ritualistic fervour, it gyrates its immense physique in vibrant ecstasy and then sinks into the depths without a trace to await its unsuspecting victims. Folklore says that the Cobra Grande is capable of changing form – one of its guises being a ghost ship, complete with searchlight. In June 1995, botanist Grace Rebelo Dos Santos saw two lights appear in the middle of the river, from a place where, earlier that evening a dragnet had become caught on something very heavy, which subsequently escaped.

'It came right close to the bank, then disappeared,' she recalled. 'The lights were like torches, about 15 inches (38 cm) apart. I'm not going to say it was a Cobra Grande, but I remember clearly how blue the lights were, which I thought very strange.'

Just where in all of this is the dividing line between fact and fiction? Well, in 1907 the famous explorer, Major Percy Fawcett, allegedly, shot a 62-foot (19 m) anaconda, and the renowned Dr Bernard Heuvelmans, famous for his book *On the Track of Unknown Animals*, described how a member of his 1947 expedition discovered a 75-foot (23 m) anaconda!

What makes the Cobra Grande so astonishing is its amazing girth. I mean, 3 feet (1 m) in diameter is pretty impressive! Part of a Cobra Grande's skeleton is said to have been discovered on the banks of the Rio Negro. The skull was reported to be more than 20 inches (51 cm) long!

Tales of the Cobra Grande pulling canoes underwater are legion. But what about these horns? It's true that large anacondas have been observed swallowing deer and other horned animals feet-first, and that at the latter stage of this progress the horns stick out from the snake's mouth, thus giving it the appearance of a horned beast. Of course once the powerful stomach acids come into play the body of its prey is quickly digested and the indigestible horns fall to the ground. But the argument that this explains the sightings has its drawbacks, for it is well known that snakes become lethargic and sleepy once they have consumed their victims, whereas the Cobra Grande, with its sinister horns intact, is always reported to be terrifying and aggressive in its actions.

The denizens of the deep constantly surprise us with their size. In the remote murky white-water rivers of Amazonia, where visibility is poor, exceptional individuals, in exceptional circumstances, could possibly reach three to four times the accepted norm. A Kamaracoto Indian vividly described to me how he had witnessed a large snake crush a full-grown jaguar to death.

If that is not enough, my patient reader, to top it all, I understand that several expeditions have been mounted in the tropical jungle of the Amazon Basin, where tribesmen speak of a large animal that walks on its hind legs and eats small trees. Dubbed the Amazonian Bigfoot, scientists believe it is a giant sloth which they thought had become extinct some 8,500 years ago.

> *I'm a reliable witness, you're a reliable witness, practically all God's*
> *children are reliable witnesses in their own estimation – which makes*
> *it funny how such different ideas of the same affair get about.*
>
> John Wyndham, *The Kraken Wakes*

Well, ladies and gentlemen, the mind boggles! There you have it! Monstrous snakes, giant sloths, and prehistoric dinosaurs!

Make of this what you will, dear reader.

As you can see my head was on fire at this point in the journey with legends, dreams and dreads.

As I sat back in my seat and closed my eyes, the words of Paul Theroux hummed in the ancient reptilian part of my brain:

> *She began nightly to dream of Octopi, sinister brownies, hobs, monital*
> *lizards, jotuns, autocthons, kleagles, lapiths, bonicons, and nests of*
> *nonnies.*
>
> *The Happy Isles of Oceania*

I half opened my eyes and quietly sang a zany song from my youth:

> *'Close the doors they're coming through the windows,*
> *Close the doors they're walking up the stairs,*
> *Close the doors they're coming down the chimney,*
> *Those ee-ee-ee-ee-ee, are everywhere!*

Having completed this promising nomination for the Eurovision Song Contest, I adjusted my seat position and fell fast asleep. Twenty minutes later I gently woke up from this refreshing smooze and helped myself to a can of orange.

Stretching my arms out in blissful content, I concluded that 'God was in his Heaven and all was right with the world'. In fact I expounded on the theme (much to the delight of Anthony) and spoke the words of that great explorer, Baron von Humboldt.

> *The most important result of all thoughtful exploration, is to recognize in the apparent confusion and opulence of nature a quintessential unity – to study each detail thoroughly yet never to be defeated by the contradictions of a mass of fact, to remember the elevated destiny of Homo sapiens and thereby to grasp the spirit of nature, its essential meaning which lies concealed under a blanket of multifarious manifestations.*
>
> *The Voyages of Humboldt and Bonpland*

After this, Anthony gave me an appreciative nod and I sat down happily with all the humility of Toad of Toad Hall.

It was noticeable that the afternoon light was fading fast. I was seated three-quarters of the way up the left-hand side of the plane, with the wing and the engine slightly in advance of my window. The plane was making good progress and we all felt it would reach Caracas before nightfall. With that reassuring thought I once more closed my eyes and enjoyed forty winks. But when I awoke I had the distinct impression that the propeller on my side of the plane had lost some of its momentum.

A young man was seated directly in front of me. His name was Nick Moss and he was married to a pretty young lady called Marianne who was seated across the gangway to the right. Nick was tall and handsome and had performed out-standingly on the expedition. Ruffling his hair I said to him, 'Nick, am I right or am I right? Do you get the feeling that the propeller is slowing down?'

'You are right,' he replied sombrely, 'I've been observing it for some time, there's something wrong with it, and the situation doesn't look too good.'

No one on our right seemed to be aware of it, and so as not to cause any alarm we both kept our peace. We were both hoping it was a minor blip and would soon rectify itself.

I'm afraid our hopes were misplaced for the engine continued to mal-function. My eyes flashed to the engine on the right. That one, thank God, seemed OK but the one on my left continued to deteriorate alarmingly, yet, strangely enough the slowly rotating blades of the engine had an almost hypnotic effect on me. They reflected the sinking sun's rays through my window into the cabin, and hummed, 'Don't worry, we're just having a rest. There's no danger, we'll start up again in a while.'

The people on my right were not aware of our predicament and were still listening enraptured to some of Anthony's stories.

Finally, the engine ceased to function altogether and Nick and I saw that the blades had stopped turning.

'The engine on the left has packed it in,' Nick announced to the whole cabin.

Despite the reassuring drone of the other engine we all froze. Time stood still!

We turned into statues. The only discernible movement was each person's eyes swinging wildly from side to side, and at this precise moment Anthony entered the record books for famous one-liners with, 'This has never happened before.'

'Really Anthony?' I replied, 'You surprise me. I thought it was all part of the service!'

There was no doubt at all that we were in a very serious situation. We were flying at 9,000 feet (2,700 m) and to our left were low-lying mountains and hills. We would have to fly over these to reach Caracas. We were still about an hour from our destination.

There was no sign of panic from the two pilots, but they were clearly very worried. My heart skipped a beat! We were very high! If the other engine should suddenly fail we would fall out of the sky like a stone and be smashed to smithereens on the rocky terrain below. I whispered as much to Nick.

'They ought to lose height and get away from those mountains and ditch in soft ground somewhere.'

Much to my relief the pilots veered away from the mountains and headed towards the greenery of the rain forest over to the right. Everyone was aware now that the pilots' only concern was to find an appropriate place to land safely. More easily said than done.

We descended to about 4,000 feet (1,200 m) but Captain Urdaneta simply couldn't find a space big enough to land. In spite of the friendlier terrain we realized what a terrifying prospect it would be to land on bushes and trees at 100 miles per hour (161 kph), or so. At best the plane would be torn apart, at worst it would simply blow up.

Half an hour passed, and the now agitated Captain was on his feet desperately searching from right to left for that elusive clearing. Half an hour is a long time to contemplate one's death! I looked around the cabin and everyone seemed quite calm. It was the same courage and fortitude that I had seen from these fine youngsters on the expedition but their eyes betrayed their apprehension and fear, which was perfectly understandable. Also among the ten youngsters were three married couples who were blissfully in love! All young people for God's sake! With all their lives in front of them.

Anthony himself was engaged. In fact, come to think of it, everybody was in love! Even I was in love!

That's right, the 'Old Hairy Yeti'. I don't need that stupid blue pill, plenty of sex and drive left in me I can tell you! We all had so much to live for. I felt so upset for the others, they didn't deserve this. It was all right for me, I was 62 years old and had lived a good fruitful life. I was frightened, make no mistake about that, and I had not yet made adequate provision for my darling wife and daughter. That thought totally overwhelmed and saddened me. But what could I do?

This feeling of helplessness almost made me laugh. It was a joke! A farce! It wasn't really happening, was it?

Whenever I have experienced death in my life, for instance when my younger brother and then my mother died, I always wanted to punch that black figure, with his stupid sickle, straight on the 'hooter'! If only I could be out of the plane, I thought to myself, with my feet firmly on the ground facing death square on with a pair of boxing gloves, I'd knock him straight into the middle of next week.

It all sounds insane, I know, but my mind was racing. My frustration grew with every fleeting moment. God in heaven! How bloody boring, I thought, to die in a poky little aeroplane. Ridiculously, I fantasized about dying on some holy quest alongside Sir Galahad. This image was then replaced by another as I saw myself reach the summit of Mount Everest with bleeding, broken legs. I imagined sacrificing my life fighting a lion in a Roman arena to save my wife and child.

Then reality bought me back to my senses. The jarring, guttural voice of Captain Ismail Urdaneta rang out across the cabin:

'Strap your seat-belts on! Emergency! Emergency!'

We were about 1,000 feet (300 m) above the trees, and because of this the impression of speed was much greater than that experienced higher in the sky. The plane lurched horribly to the right and dipped precariously downwards.

There was a look of abject terror in the eyes of one of the ladies.

'It's all right,' shouted Nick, 'they'll get us down safely.'

All I could see through my window was jungle. Was Urdaneta going to land us on that or had he, at last, found a clearing? Though his co-pilot was sitting down, he was still standing. From this position he had one hand on the controls and the other on a hand-mike. Into this he shouted, 'Mayday! Mayday! Emergency! Emergency!' and lots of other jargon which I didn't understand. What was alarming was the fact that he was still standing! I could see that he was still searching for a suitable place to land. The poor man was distraught and sweating profusely, yet he still appeared in control of the situation.

It seemed the plane was probably running out of fuel, or that the remaining engine was beginning to malfunction. It was spluttering, but, of course, the Captain may have been shutting it down to redress the balance for a glided landing.

To my delight, large patches of greenery appeared between the trees, but we were still going very fast and the scenery whizzed by at an alarming rate.

Suddenly I had the weird sensation of weightlessness as the plane dropped 50 feet (15 m) or so. We started to dip sharply to the right. Jesus! It was dramatic! And then all hell broke loose! It reminded me of the moment in the film *Apollo 13* when Tom Hanks said from the immense void of space, 'Houston, we have a problem.'

We certainly had a problem. Noises that reminded me of anti-aircraft ack-ack guns, blasted out from the instrument control panel. This unnerving sound finally confirmed to our stunned minds the fact that we really were going to crash.

Orange lights started flashing on and off as if we had won a top prize on a television game show. I was almost tempted to shout, 'Ismail Urdaneta, Come On Down.' Down, down, down we went, and up, up, up came the ground to meet us! I just felt cold and stubborn. No, I thought, I'm damned if I am going to die like this!

I sat myself on the empty seat to my right away from the window and secured the seat-belt, and gripped the back of the seat in front of me. People's voices seemed far away and I felt as if I was moving in a slow motion dream. Across the gangway was a young lady called Janet, who enquired in a matter-of-fact sort of way:

'Brian, what's the brace position?'

I smiled back at her and said, 'Oh sweetheart, just get your head down and hold on to the seat in front of you.'

She did just that, but not before exchanging a loving look with her husband Miles, who was seated behind her.

In front of me on the left the veins on Nick's neck stood out like telegraph wires as he strained his head around to catch a glimpse of his wife, Marianne. She was at the rear of the plane with Anthony, her lips opening and closing in consternation as she returned his gaze. Everyone else seemed to be in the brace position. The remaining married couple, Tim and Karen, were bent over and holding hands. On seeing me sitting upright Anthony shouted, 'Brace yourself, Challenger.'

The instruction was taken up by Captain Urdaneta as he finally sat down.

This is it! I thought. This is it! Brace yourselves! I ask you! It all seemed too daft to laugh at.

My mind conjured up the image of Rocky Marciano. (Bear with me! I promise you I haven't lost the plot.) Rocky Marciano? Well, in the early 1950s Marciano was the heavyweight boxing champion of the world. He was 5 feet 10 inches (1.8 m) tall and weighed 13 stone 5.5 pounds (85 km). Every challenger he fought was bigger than he was, yet with his awesome power, he terrified and destroyed them all. His famous right hand, which kissed all comers asleep, was affectionately known as the 'Suzy Q'. He was unbeaten for the whole of his career and he was considered indestructible. At the age of 49 he died in a plane crash in the USA. The plane was a small Cessna, not dissimilar in size to the one we were flying. When aviation experts examined the wreckage they found Marciano contorted and mangled in the metal fuselage. His body was discovered in the perfect brace position.

What chance had we got, I thought, if a guy as powerful as Marciano had ended up compressed like a concertina!

With this cheerful thought in my head, we hit the ground. It was a dreadful moment. Bang, thud, wallop! God knows how to describe the sound and to be perfectly honest I can't remember what it sounded like, I simply felt as sick as a dog. Adrenalin surged through my body. Yes, we were down, thank God. And miraculously still in one piece. The pilots deserved a lot of brownie points for that.

We were careering along a field of thick high grass like an out-of-control express train. We really were going at a hell of a lick. The scenery outside my window was a blur. The plane shook violently as the two heroic pilots fought desperately to control it. The great danger was that once it stopped the tail end would flip over and cause it to explode. But, thank our lucky stars, this didn't happen.

There was a tremendous thud and the plane came to an abrupt standstill. The impact was so great that I actually tore the seat I was hanging on to out of the floor!

Someone yelled, 'Get out quickly – it can blow up at any minute.'

The ladies went first, jettisoning themselves into the long grass and we, the chaps, followed in quick succession.

'Keep going. Keep going,' urged Nick, 'to hell with the bloody luggage, leave it, it's not important. We have got to get well away from the plane. I've seen one blow up!'

This was all very well and good, but we had landed in a swampy field and were up to our knees in mud and water. This, combined with the long, thick grass, made our progress painfully slow. However, eventually, we reached a safe distance from the plane.

Our commotion through the swamp stirred up clouds of mosquitoes and other 'dive bombers', which set about us with a vengeance. Once more we sampled *el sudar y las moscas*.

These insect swarms were frightful. The mosquitoes seemed to have proboscises long and tough enough to pierce bell metal. My bare forearms quickly became a bloody mess, but it was the ladies who suffered the most, Marianne in particular. Thinking that the expedition was over they had not put on their long trousers or protective shirts. Much to Marianne's distress, lumps and bumps appeared all over her arms and legs.

This was all too much, coming so quickly after the crash. We were a group of terrified people in shock. The women wept openly and the men were bent double in an effort to control their emotions. I stood shaking, my video camera in my hand. Andrew Bawn, a delightful Scotsman exclaimed, 'Bloody hell, Brian, do you mean to say that you have been filming it all?'

'Yes,' I nodded.

He shook his head in absolute disbelief, 'God, you're a cool bugger!'

'Not at all,' I replied, 'I always knew that we would get down safely!'

'Yes,' said Andrew, 'And liars are born every minute.'

To which I replied, 'Yes – and this one was born sixty-two years ago.'

We laughed in indescribable relief.

It was then that we realized to our utter amazement that the two pilots had remained beside the aircraft. They stood motionless outside the exit door.

'They're bloody fools,' said Nick, 'they could have been killed.'

After a while, Anthony decided to have a word with them. He set off towards the plane. Meanwhile the sky had filled with tiny white aeroplanes responding to Captain Urdaneta's distress calls. Though there was nothing they could do to assist us, the sight of them cheered us up immensely. We waved enthusiastically to show that we were all right and they continued to circle round. The planes looked so pretty against the dark blue sky. To any Pemon Indians observing them from afar they must have looked like a host of giant white butterflies in search of sweet scented orchids. The 'orchids' of course were us – and we 'orchids' needed to get a move on. It was 6.30 in the evening and getting dark, and the mosquitoes were increasing in number by the minute.

At this point Anthony beckoned to us shouting, 'It's all right. The Captain says that the plane is safe. It won't blow up. Come and get your luggage and we'll start walking out of here.'

The decision to walk was welcomed by all and was certainly preferable to sitting around in the dark being bitten to death. So ten minutes later we had on our backpacks and were on the move.

Anthony started talking to a friendly Pemon Indian farmer who owned the field that we had landed in and, despite the fact that the plane had damaged a considerable portion of his land, he was sweetness and light. The pilots told us that he would be well compensated and I got the impression that the farmer was actually enjoying every minute of the excitement. It was obviously something he could tell his grandchildren for years to come. Justifiably so – the plane had almost hit him!

Apparently he had been watching it for some time when it suddenly started to head towards him. In blind panic he began to run round his field like the famous ouzel bird, which you may or may not know is a legendary bird which eventually disappeared up its own arse! Finally, in sheer desperation, he ran for the nearest ditch and took a header into it. It must have looked comical to the mosquitoes!

Anyway, he appeared to be none the worse for his brush with death and guided us for the next half-hour. He took us to a rough track which led to a farm and the beginnings of civilization. Without his help we might have gone in the opposite direction and spent hours in the rain forest. The sense of relief we all felt was plain. It was good to be alive.

The happy Pemon Indian now introduced us to the owner of the farm. He was a big corpulent man in his early 40s with lots of children and an equally corpulent wife. They looked happy. I have a feeling that Venezuela is probably the happiest country in the world. Christopher Columbus was the first Westerner to lay eyes on it and was overwhelmed by its beauty. He called it 'The Land of Grace', and named the inhabitants 'Indians', and the misnomer has stuck (although in Spanish, native Venezuelans now prefer to be referred to as *Indgenas* or 'Indigenous' people. Well, there was no doubt at all that the 'Indigenous' farmer and his family were astonished to see us – after all we had literally fallen out of the sky. They certainly found my hairy appearance hilarious, the children in particular were delighted when I produced a series of low growls. My imitation of a 'woolly yeti' brought a new character on to the scene who was not in the least bit impressed by my atavistic behaviour – I couldn't believe my eyes. It was a Jack Russell terrier!

I have to tell you that back in England, I possess, among my many animals a Jack Russell called Duke. He completely dominates my life and I love him to death, but he bullies me from dawn till dusk. If I don't do as he wants, he makes my life a misery. You will have heard the term 'she who must be obeyed', well Duke is 'he who must be obeyed'! You can therefore understand my consternation at being confronted by a Jack Russell in deepest Venezuela. I mean Jack Russells mainly inhabit Yorkshire and Lancashire and Rick Stein's restaurant in pretty Padstow, but surely not the wilds of Venezuela.

I rubbed my eyes to see if I was imagining things, after all shamans (witch doctors) abound in this mysterious continent and one of them may have cast a spell on me and brought forth 'he who must be obeyed'. But on closer inspection I gratefully discovered that this was not the case, for the Venezuelan Jack Russell was brown and white and covered in dry cow dung, whereas Duke, back in Bagshot, England was black and white and occasionally covered in horse manure. Nevertheless, my fearsome adversary gave a good account of himself (much to the glee of the children) and chased the 'yeti' out of the farmyard. This fine achievement seemed to gratify his ego and he turned round as proud as punch and retired peacefully to the confines of the house.

Whilst I had been enjoying this little escapade, Anthony had discovered where we were. Apparently, we had landed in the neighbourhood of Lagartijo Reservoir, situated in the Tuy Valley, about 2.5 hours' drive from Caracas. We were also pleased to hear that we were only twenty minutes away from a busy road. It all sounded very encouraging and, after I had taken a quick group photograph, we said farewell to the farmer and his family and headed down a rough pathway in the direction of the road.

It was about 7.30 p.m. now and almost dark. The road, when we reached it, positively buzzed with activity, horses and carts, beaten up old vans and noisy bangers whizzed by and we became very hopeful of a lift. As if on cue a large school bus approached from around the corner and the two pilots waved it down. After a quick consultation with the driver we all piled on board and waved a hurried goodbye to the heroic Pemon Indian.

One or two seats were free for the ladies, otherwise the bus was loaded with giggling schoolchildren, aged between 10 and 15, dressed in smart brown and yellow uniforms. We must have looked a sight. I was covered in mud and flies and looked particularly impressive. I caught a glimpse of my reflection in one of the windows and thought I bore a striking resemblance to the fabled 'skunk ape' who is supposed to live in the Florida Everglades.

As we motored along, the children sang a song which reminded me of the ditty 'One Man Went to Mow'. And though they were singing in Spanish I found it easy to join in, which amused them enormously.

This happy jaunt lasted for about half an hour and then we disembarked outside a bus station and Anthony went off to phone for assistance. He returned with the good news that he had organized a special bus to take us on to Caracas. He had also phoned our operative at the hotel to let him know that we were all right as our crash landing had made the evening news.

The bus arrived and Anthony urged us on board, as it was clear that we had all lost the spring in our step and were becoming weary and somewhat sluggish! After a few minutes however, we were all safely on board and heading for Caracas. This journey was, thank goodness, uneventful and two hours later we arrived at the hotel in a subdued mood.

According to the National Restaurant Owners Association, Caracas has more restaurants per capita than any other city in Latin America, and once we had checked into the hotel, Anthony, took us to one called Basillo. The décor was of a rain forest and jungle sounds emanated from every corner with picturesque waterfalls cascading down limestone rocks into clear pools of delight. A fine collection of tropical plans adorned every nook and cranny, and painted toucans, parrots and macaws stood out comically against the emerald background. The ambience of the place was absolutely captivating and one could not have wished for a finer setting in which to end our adventure. The service, too was superb and liberal quantities of alcohol were consumed as the conversation flowed across a very noisy dining table.

It was great to see everyone relaxed and happy and gradually the nightmare of the crash landing receded from our thoughts. By God we were so hungry we could have eaten the arse of a plesiosaur!

So what did we eat after three weeks in the jungle plus an unexpected trip to death's door? We sampled everything the restaurant had to offer, including *cachapa*, a thick, slightly sweet pancake made with maize, and Venezuela's national dish, *pabellon criollo*, made from shredded beef spiced with onions, green pepper, tomato, coriander, garlic, white rice, a scoop of *caraotas negras* (black beans) and strips of fried plantain. We followed this with an irresistible sweet called *chorros* which is crispy fried pastry tubes sprinkled with sugar and served with hot chocolate. Absolutely delicious! To top it all off we were then served the *pièce de résistance*, Venezuela's most distinctive dessert – *bienmesabe*. This dreamy desert is a sponge cake doused in coconut cream. Yum, yum, yum! *Bienmesabe* translates as 'tastes good to me', and to say its rich is to put it very mildly!

Finally, the coffee. Venezuela is a nation of coffee worshippers and it is more than just a drink, it is an integral part of the Venezuelan way of life. Rich, aromatic and always fresh, each cup is brewed to order. They would not dream of letting a pot languish on a hotplate. And so I ordered a huge glass of cappuccino, smothered in fresh whipped cream. By the end of the evening I could hardly walk.

Our happy-go-lucky expedition bus driver, a stocky man in his mid-50s called Silva, joked that beer drinking is Venezuela's national sport. Venezuela has two main brands of beer. The best-selling is Polar, which for years has been exported in refrigerated containers to ensure freshness. Nacional is the other, and is a more working-class drink. A beer called Brahma Chopp has recently been introduced from Brazil but it has to be said that Polar is the bestseller.

Silva said to me, 'Brian, on a hot night like tonight, you ask for "cerveza bein fria", meaning you want Polar just short of frozen!'

I discovered that Venezuelans rarely choose clear drinks like vodka and gin. No! Rum is their passion. Rum, matey! Rum! I recounted to Silva how I had played Long John Silver in a 10-part TV series for the Walt Disney Corporation entitled *Return to Treasure Island*. Of course, Long John's favourite drink was rum.

'We filmed the series in Jamaica,' I continued. 'The rum there was fantastic!'

Silva slowly took this on board, and then with great intensity replied, 'The finest rum in the world is here in Venezuela.'

I smiled back at him. God! I thought, I love this man.

Two kindred spirits, Silva and I had whistled and sung songs together across the greater part of the Gran Sabana. He gestured dramatically to the waiter and two ticks later a large glass full of pinkish liquid was placed in front of me.

'Before you drink, Brian,' he whispered, 'let me tell you that we Venezuelans drink rum with cola, with fruit juice, with *aguakina* (tonic water), or with angostura bitters, invented in the Orinoco port city of Angostura. Sometimes we also drink it with ice and fresh lime slices, but our favourite and most delicious concoction is *ron con parchita* – rum with passion fruit. That, Brian is the drink that is now in front of you. Drink it slowly and dream of paradise, dream of the savannah and its beautiful sunburnt immensity!'

As we got back to the hotel, Silva put an arm around me and said, 'Brian, if you have a *ratoncito* [hangover] tomorrow morning don't take an aspirin, there is only one cure – ask the hotel to serve you a steaming bowl of *mondongo* [tripe soup] – that will cure you.'

'Cure or kill,' I replied. 'Thank you for that helpful advice, Silva, that's cheered me up enormously. I will look forward to tomorrow. Maybe you could join me for breakfast and we can sample the tripe soup together?'

'Ah, Brian,' smiled Silva, 'I would love to, but I never get a hangover.'

I smiled back at him and after pinching his nose, repeated, 'See you tomorrow for breakfast!'

He laughed and mounted the steps of his cherished bus and sped away into the night. As I watched it disappear, I felt a friendly hand on my shoulder. It was a young fair-haired man called David Gardiner a member of our expedition.

David was a rather intense, private man, who in spite of a damaged shoulder, had performed splendidly on the expedition.

We drew breath together and embraced the silence that had fallen. Our gaze took in the distant neon lights of Caracas. He murmured, 'What a day, eh Brian? What an adventure we've had these last few weeks! What an adventure!'

'Yes indeed, David,' I replied. 'And you've shown a lot of guts. Everyone is very impressed with you.'

His face lit up and we turned and made our way into the hotel to join the others. Standing in the doorway were the two airline pilots and I was surprised to see them so late. They seemed sad.

'Have you had something to eat?' I enquired.

Both men nodded and smiled and then became sad again. I gathered that they had been through a rather torrid time answering questions from the Ministry of Transport and filling in various forms. It is standard practice in Venezuela that if you crash-land a plane you are automatically grounded for six months, pending an investigation. Poor chaps, I felt really sorry for them and shook their hands and thanked them for saving our lives. Whatever the outcome of the official report in the weeks to come, there was no denying that the two pilots had performed brilliantly. Bringing that plane down safely in that terrain was a miracle. For my money Captain Urdaneta took the right decision when he decided to make an emergency landing, and much to his delight, I told him so. We all shook them by the hand and hugged and kissed them and they went on their way in a much happier frame of mind.

I retired to my room and treated myself to a long cold shower. God! It was hot! My whole body was on fire. The truth is I very rarely drink, and Silva's rums had knocked me sideways. I lay on the bed and the room spun slowly round and round.

Through the large open window I looked out at the beautiful night sky. The stars shone with a rare density. The Milky Way, with its gracious curve, dominated the glare of Caracas' city lights. Its dense tapestry of glowing stars shone in blue, yellow, green, white and red. Orion, with its outriders, lit the blanket of the night with dazzling brightness. The planet Venus was so large in the sky that it cast shadows in my bedroom. This mysterious planet reminded me of the Lost World, for many of the *tepuis* are hidden by dense cloud cover, rather like the surface clouds of Venus. Images of the rain and cloud forests hummed around my brain and then evaporated into the magic of the night. There was no doubt at all that I was 'sozzled'!

As I lay perspiring on my bed, my mind began to ferment with nostalgia for my childhood. That's where it had all begun.

PART ONE

CHILDHOOD DREAMS

1

STRANG THE TERRIBLE

From my earliest days, epic stories of great adventure would stir my imagination and leave me begging for more.

Home was 30 Probert Avenue, Goldthorpe near Rotherham, South Yorkshire. The avenue itself was part of a circle that contained a hundred houses or more. The whole place was full of trees and high hedges, forming a labyrinth of hidden dens and pathways.

The small road was lit by old-fashioned gas-lamps, which cast mysterious shadows in the gathering dusk. The landscape was the perfect setting for a million escapades. These were the exciting years of the early 1940s and I was 7 years old.

Like hordes of bees, my buddies and I would pour across the street, rush through numerous hidden pathways and people's back gardens, until we arrived at our favourite destination: the old disused railway embankment.

We had never, ever seen a train use it. Thick with rust, the line was fading away and the wooden sleepers were rotten. A large iron bridge connected one embankment to the other. This magnificent structure was the focal point of our frenzied activity. The gang of lads I belonged to was second to none. Brave lads and true!

This was our fantasy land, full of fire-breathing dragons, swamps infested with savage crocodiles, man-eating sharks and flesh-hungry piranhas. There were bloodthirsty vampire bats, invaders from the red planet Mars and armies of green treen warriors led by the evil Mekon from the Dan Dare picture strip in the *Eagle* comic. Then there were cowboys like Gene Autrey, Johny Mack Brown, Zorro, and my personal favourite, Hopalong Cassidy.

Directly opposite the embankment, beyond some intervening houses, was another railway line. This one, in contrast to the other, was fully alive and active, for this was part of the Great North Eastern Railway.

On many summer afternoons, we would sit at the back of a friendly neighbour's house, steaming engines go by – goods trains, struggling with all their might to pull iron wagons loaded with ore. On rainy days the engines would seem to bend and groan with the effort. Sparks flew as the wheels ran free, unable to grip the wet track.

All the while, the sweating stokers, their faces lit by the fire in the furnace, would be shovelling coal ten to the dozen in an effort to sustain the drive. The roar of the frustrated engine, and the massive eruptions of grey-black smoke from the funnel, like some belaboured dragon, compelled us to assist the magnificent effort by cheering them to the rooftops.

This would be greeted by a broad smile from the grimy face of the driver, as he raised his GNER hat in approval, and sounded his shrill whistle.

Gradually, the skill of the driver and the titanic efforts of the stokers would win the day, and the metal beast would gather pace and power away.

My Father, William Blessed, was a coal miner, like most men in the area, and worked at Hickleton Main Colliery, one of the largest pits in South Yorkshire. His shift at work started at 6.00 in the morning, which meant he had to rise at 4.30 and finish at 1.30 in the afternoon. In his spare time he was the opening fast bowler for Bolton-on-Dearne in the prestigious Yorkshire Cricket League. I adored him! It goes without saying that I had 'The Best Mum in the World'. She attended to my every need, whether it be iodine for my pugilistic wounds, or medicine for the usual long line of illnesses that my generation was subject to. She was an angel.

The centre of Goldthorpe was half a mile away, and at its heart were two cinema houses. One was the Empire, and the other the Picture House.

At each cinema, there was what was known as a first house, which started at 5.00 p.m., and a second which started at 8.00 p.m. These citadels of entertainment were tremendously popular. It was not an uncommon sight to see people queuing for hundreds of yards to see the latest films.

But Saturday morning was the kids' matinée, by far the grandest time of the week. I would leap out of bed, full of joy and anticipation at the magic that I knew lay ahead. The big thrill would come at midday, the appointed hour for the next episode of *Flash Gordon*, starring Buster Crabbe.

'Ah tha comin' to the pictures?' echoed the chorus of voices of the kids in my street.

I joined them from my garden by leaping over an enormous hedge. Being small and light, it was easy to somersault over it and land on my feet. A round of applause always greeted my landing.

'I wish I could do that,' said an old man passing by.

'You'll break your neck one of these days!'

'No I won't,' I shouted, 'because I'm Vultan, King of the Hawkmen from *Flash Gordon*.'

Little did I realize that one day I would actually play the part in a remake of the film.

Anyway, the sun was high, and the cinema was beckoning. We ran down the Goldthorpe Road at breakneck speed and there was the centre of the galaxy, our place of worship, the temple itself: the marvellous, wondrous, magnificent Picture House. It seemed to take forever to get inside because the queue was always so long, but at last the moment arrived. There we all were, gazing up at the screen, waiting with baited breath for the projector to whirr into life.

Then the lights went out and the screen lit up as the curtains were pulled back. Mickey Mouse walked on to the screen to thunderous applause. But, after all too brief a time, the cartoons were over, 'That's All Folks!'

Next, heralded by the trumpeting of a crowing cockerel, it was the 'Pathé Newsreel'. This was put together with a younger audience in mind. No politics here: football matches. Manchester United, Wolverhampton Wanderers, the England goalkeeper with huge hands, Frank Swift. It would end with a few brief shots of the King and Queen. Then we knew that what we'd all been waiting for was only minutes away.

The curtains closed while the projectionist changed reels. How could Flash have possibly survived? Surely not this time. He was doomed, or was he? Everyone was on the edge of their seats as the curtains drew back once again to reveal space rockets zooming across the sky.

A replay. Flash falling down a cavernous pit. What's going to happen? A button is pressed and a net swings out, catching him just in time and saving him from certain death.

The episode reached its wonderfully thrilling climax; a gigantic lizard monster had Flash in a deadly death hold. All the life was slowly being crushed out of him. Death was inevitable.

Oh God. How we wanted the film to keep going. Alas, this was not to be. Lights around us flashed red, and it was time to go till next week. We all trudged out at the management's insistence, dejected, but avidly discussing the events we'd just witnessed avidly.

'How about that monster!' I said to the elder of our gang.

'That was a dinosaur,' he replied. 'They lived on the Earth millions of years ago.'

'Were they really so big?'

'Bigger than an elephant,' he whispered.

I was staggered.

I had an even bigger shock when my dad took me to see the epic film *King Kong*. This experience completely blew my mind. I would sit on the railway embankment, like a moonstruck calf, dreaming of that magnificent giant gorilla and his prehistoric homeland. I loved his great shoulders and barrel chest, which he kept thumping with immense pride. But what really excited me was his battle with the Tyrannosaurus rex. During a pause in the fight the tyrannosaurus actually scratched its ear! I thought that was magical.

The last scene where King Kong falls from the Empire State Building, having been shot from the circling aeroplanes, left me feeling wretched. On the way home I was inconsolable.

'Why did he have to die, Dad?' I sobbed. 'Why did they take him to New York? Why didn't they leave him alone in the jungle?'

'It's all right, lad,' Dad replied, stroking my forehead. 'After all, he did manage to knock one of the planes out of the sky. Those pilots didn't 'ave it all their own way.'

'That's right, Dad,' I sobbed, cheering up a bit. 'Serves them right. I'll bet you a ton of marbles that if those pilots hadn't been in their aeroplanes, King Kong would 'ave multi-crushed them!' This made my father laugh, and we carried on home in much happier spirits.

After seeing *King Kong*, I became totally obsessed with dinosaurs. Day in, day out, I would drive my parents potty with questions about their existence. I had such a deep yearning to see them. It was heart-breaking to hear that they no longer roamed the Earth. In my heart of hearts, I felt quite certain that a few still remained.

Any talks on the radio about these creatures would command all of my attention and lift my spirits. I would listen to explorers on the cherished BBC

Home Service, describing what the Earth must have been like millions of years ago: the air much thicker and syrupy, as a result of the luxuriant gigantic trees and plants. At school I would bombard the poor teachers with feverish questions about the various sizes of dinosaurs.

'Which was the biggest, Sir?' 'Which was the longest?' 'Which was the fastest?' 'How fast could they run?' 'Which was the tallest?' 'How many dinosaurs could Tyrannosaurus rex fight?' 'What colour was their skin?' 'Could an armour-plated ankylosaurus beat a Russian T4 tank, Sir?' 'Why did they die, Sir?' 'What killed them?' 'I don't believe they are dead. "Lenny the Dwarf" told me that there's one alive in a lake in Scotland! We ought to go and 'ave a look!'

In 1944, when I was 8 years old, my dad gave me the welcome news that I could have his air-raid shelter.

'You can 'ave it, lad. It's no use, it lets water in.'

The news thrilled me to bits.

'But what if we get bombed, Dad?'

He shrugged.

'Don't worry, Brian, lad. This house is solid, and they'll probably only bomb Sheffield and places like that. The most we're gonna get is a bit of shrapnel.'

Certainly, after rainy days, the shelter did ship quite a lot of water, though it was only a few inches deep and soon soaked away. It was the perfect place to hide away and keep my old pots, pans and my makeshift aquarium. The terrible creatures that I possessed – natterjacks and common toads, frogs, smooth newts and great crested newts – earned me the nickname of Baron Frankenstein.

Many adults couldn't understand my preoccupation with them, and voiced the opinion that it was unnatural. My parents, however, were sympathetic and encouraged my hobby. Although my mother did berate me for allowing a great crested newt to walk across the living room floor, and cause our next-door neighbour, Mrs Burns, to scream and leave the house.

At about this time I was besotted with a character from the *Beano* comic called Strang the Terrible. Dressed in a leopard-skin, Strang was a giant of a man who carried a great club and was always accompanied by a large pet dinosaur. Puffing my chest out with false pride I boastfully proclaimed to the local children that Strang periodically stayed in our house and that his dinosaur lived downstairs in our large cellar and was fed on turnips. They believed me and I, encouraged by their gullibility, expanded on this theme. I told them with macabre delight that my cellar was connected to a large tunnel that ran under all their houses and led to a gigantic underground prehistoric world that was lit by bright minerals. There were great holes in this strange kingdom, which led to the centre of the Earth. I described how hundreds of dinosaurs used the tunnels for exercise. If they should feel tremors now and then under their houses, they were not to be frightened because the council had built them with strong bricks. If any of the dinosaurs should become bad tempered, Strang the Terrible would easily soothe them by playing sweetly on his 'pan's pipes'. If that didn't work, he would hit them over the head with his club. In the unlikely event of a stegosaurus sticking its head through one of their pantry floors, they should call on me and I would arrange for Strang to sort it out.

These stories went on for weeks, and gave the children nightmares. I hasten to add that all the children were older than me. It wasn't in my nature to frighten babies. But the parents, as you can imagine, were furious. A large group of them came to our front door one day and made a formal complaint about me. They strongly urged my dad to give me a thrashing and send me to bed without any supper. Some of them actually wanted to witness the punishment. In fact, some of them were keen to administer the belt themselves.

My mother was having none of it, and I had my cricket bat in my hands ready to bash their shins. I'm not naming names in this story but one bad-tempered bald man from across the street shouted, 'Your son Brian, is a bloody liar, and he should tell all these kids here that his stories about dinosaurs are a pack of lies.' I had to respond to this. The children were all there, staring at me. They believed in me. A few of them might have had nightmares, yes! But in general my stories had filled their lives with magic. They loved them, and found them inspirational. I wasn't about to take the bald man's insults lying down. 'No, don't call me a bloody liar.' I shouted back. 'You're wrong! My stories are true, it's just that you are too old to see dinosaurs.' I was glad to see my spirited reply had impressed the children, but their parents became even more incensed.

My father came to my rescue. He put up his hand and silenced them in a flash. He was a union leader and used to handling crowds. 'I've never hit Brian in my life,' he said quietly, 'and I'm not about to start now. So if it's a belting you want to see, I'm afraid you're going to have to go elsewhere. You go about your business and I'll discipline my son as I think fit.' That was the end of the matter, and after a few disgruntled murmurs the crowd retreated down the pathway and out of sight. Afterwards my mother took Dad aside into the kitchen, speaking to him in a hushed voice. It was difficult to make out what she was saying, just the occasional. 'Whatever is going to become of him, Billy,' being discernible. Several minutes later my father returned, and after a further period of deliberation, he said, 'Well, lad. If you want to tell stories, there's no harm in that. Though I think you should give the dinosaurs a rest for a while.' And then with a twinkle, he added, 'Maybe, one day, you'll invite Strang the Terrible to supper!'

And so Strang the Terrible took a long, well-deserved holiday in Outer Mongolia. Nevertheless, the children would still somehow manage to steal away to my air-raid shelter to see my intriguing collection of frogs, toads and newts and listen to my stories about giants, dragons, jungles, mountains and quicksands. None of them could resist me, and I dazzled their senses like some latter-day Pied Piper. Come to think of it, Scheherazade.

As much as I was the story-teller of our street, though, our Bush radio, in its wooden case, was my source for magical and stimulating yarns. It was the heart of the house and diverted us royally with shows on the BBC Home Service and the Light Programme. *Captain Blood, Journey to the Other Side of the Sun, Paul Temple, Dick Barton: Special Agent* and *The War of the Worlds* were favourites. But the one I loved most of all was the astonishing and evocative *The Lost World* by Sir Arthur Conan Doyle.

The dramatization of Doyle's *The Lost World* particularly fired my imagination because the actors and the special effects told the story of a mysterious landscape in South America where prehistoric monsters, unchanged since the Palaeozoic period, roamed. The story in a nutshell is as follows.

Led by the larger-than-life figure of Professor Challenger, a scientific expedition that included Lord John Roxton, Professor Summerlee and the journalist Edward Malone, sets out to explore a plateau in South America that has remained frozen in time, since the days that dinosaurs roamed the Earth. Seemingly impossible to penetrate, the Lost World holds great danger for the four men, from fiendish ape-men and terrifying prehistoric creatures. When they arrive back in Britain they are confronted by an intimidating audience, sceptical of their claims. The story reaches its climax when Professor Challenger produces evidence that dinosaurs do exist.

In 1884, the British botanist Everard im Thurn made the first ascent of Roraima. Once back in England he lectured about his expedition and one of these lectures was attended by Sir Arthur Conan Doyle. Doyle was so fascinated by this account that it inspired him to write his book *The Lost World*. The BBC's serialization certainly inspired me, and I ran thither and yon in the streets around my home in Probert Avenue, enacting the adventures of Professor Challenger and his companions to anyone and everyone I came across. They must have thought I was stark raving mad!

2

THE PIXIE

Our home was a very happy place. Unfortunately, school was another matter – Highgate Junior School, which was half a mile away in Goldthorpe. Once there, I couldn't shake off the feeling of being a stranger or, indeed, some kind of alien. Between seven and eleven is such a delicate age and the rigidity of school made me catatonic. Their rigid rules stunted my progress, and I instinctively returned to my core and quietly protected what I knew was real. In this state I was neither rude nor rebellious – simply happily silent. How sad that the teachers didn't understand that I was staring at the limitless landscape beyond, where knowledge and being meet and lead to understanding.

On the great day of my eleven-plus examination I doubt if any exam invigilator was ever as flabbergasted as ours was when I announced with great confidence after twenty minutes that I had finished. 'Are you absolutely sure, boy?' the gentleman asked, incredulously.

'Yes,' I replied, 'it was easy, Sir. A piece of cake!' The truth was, I was so impatient to get outside that I had filled the exam papers with sketches of dinosaurs, King Kong and the like. Lads like me weren't interested in exams.

So there I was, in the middle of the football field, pausing now and then to look at the purple haze on the distant horizon. Oh! How pure the air tasted. What bliss! What calm! I lingered a little longer before slowly making my way to the nearest pond.

If you follow the railway line from Probert Avenue for 2 miles (3 km) or so, nearing Bolton-on-Dearne, you arrive at the Seven Fields. In the early days of my childhood those distant pastures contained the most amazing hordes of frogs, toads and newts. The fields dipped gently, and at the lowest point there was a narrow stream, stretching for miles, that everyone called the Gam. Lining it were a wide variety of bushes and trees, in particular weeping willows. The Gam was slow-moving and held many forms of pond plants: lilies, aponogeton, marginals and oxygenating plants. Its depth varied from 2 to 4 feet (0.6–1.2 m) and it exuded total peace and perfect natural balance. Of all the places of my childhood, this one gave me the deepest peace. Of course, on many occasions I would go there with the Probert Avenue Gang and we would spend an enjoyable day. But it could never compare with being there on my own. That was complete bliss. The summer sun would shine down brightly, while a gentle breeze would stir the willows, and produce a gentle rustling music. I would blow on a hand-made whistle made from a bulrush, like some rustic child-Pan oblivious of time.

During this idyll water beetles with glistening blue-black bodies would busy themselves, hurrying up and down the stems of the lilies. Water-boatmen would skate across the surface, skilfully avoiding the caddis-flies. Newts would rise, blow an air bubble, then descend into the mysterious depths of the multicoloured weeds; newts of the most gorgeous colours – brown, light-red, yellow, orange, black and even the odd albino. The smooth skin of the female common newt, what grace! Swimming ghost-like along the marginal plants, she would leave a trail of delicate eggs.

One day a deep-lying plant parted to reveal a larger specimen: a great crested newt. I put my hand gently into the water and then, finding myself in a position to stroke it, lifted it to the surface. What I saw took my breath away. Placing it in a very large jamjar, I was able to examine the creature at my leisure. It was male, 8 inches (20 cm) long, and the most stunning great crested newt I'd ever set eyes on, with big protruding eyes, a long, black body and a crest suggesting high black pinnacles. Its stomach, by contrast, was golden with large black spots. The creature in the jar was somewhat magnified by the glass, and, held up to the sunlight, it seemed to me to symbolize all the primitive magic of the animal kingdom. Another movement and it was in my hands again; then a gentle stroke and an effortless return to the water. Down he plunged, free, his legs pressed against his body as he dived out of sight. The whole episode seemed like some secret ceremony.

As I stared at the vision, a sensation of well-being enveloped me, and I could feel my eyes focusing with ever-greater concentration. The odd green leaf or petal floated and circulated in the tiny eddies. The water's surface and what lay beneath it beckoned me, drawing me down to share in the mystery.

When the gang was with me, I would hold sway over them. 'Tell us stories, Brian,' they would beg. Slowly, in a hushed voice, I would tell stories about the great dinosaurs, using newts as a starting point. 'In the history of the Earth,' I would tell them, 'nowt was like those giants.' Then I would rattle off the names at great speed, 'Triceratops, pteranodon, antosaurus, pterodaciylus, brachadon, pliosaurus, diplodocus, allosauraus, ichthyosaurus, stegosaurus, gorgosaurus, brontosaurus and the great thunder lizard Tyrannosaurus rex! They roamed the land around here, and they were like huge newts, all different colours. It wasn't long ago that they were still alive. They died out 60 million years ago. That's not long. But I tell you what I miss,' I lamented. 'That they're not alive today . . .'

Hours passed as I described how explorers maintained that prehistoric creatures still existed in certain parts of the world. Even in Scotland there was the Loch Ness Monster. Mouths opened wide and drooled as I embellished on my theme. 'Go on, Brian . . . Go on!' they pleaded. 'Well,' I said, pausing for effect, 'we still don't know much about the Matto Gross in Brazil, and the Gran Sabana in Venezuela. That's where *The Lost World* is set. Conan Doyle calls it Maple White Land. Isn't that a lovely name? When we're a bit older, we should go there by plane, boat and then on foot, like Professor Challenger and his men. Not even head-hunters with poison darts and blowpipes, deadly snakes, anacondas that can crush a train, quicksands and high precipices should stop us from getting there . . . to Roraima!' 'Roraima? What's that?' they asked. 'I keep telling you, it's the Lost World. It really exists. Look at the map of Venezuela.' Everybody was absorbed in his own thoughts as I sat back and watched, satisfied and pleased with myself. Their imaginations were filled with dreams of magical deeds to come. Then the whole scene was ruined by a strident voice from the railway embankment. It was 9-year-old randy little Elsie Green, who was always showing me her knickers. 'Brian! . . . Brian Blessed!' Immediately I sank deeper into the long grass. 'I can see you . . . yer mother says yer tea's ready, and if you don't come this minute, she'll clear the table!'

A golden summer passed and in the autumn of 1947, I was in my eleventh year and I transferred from Highgate Junior Mixed School to Bolton-on-Dearne Secondary Modern. The regimentation of the junior school was replaced by an even sterner regime. Loud, cold comments from unfamiliar teachers and prefects echoed down the corridors: 'Keep in line!' 'No talking!' 'Hold your heads up straight, idiots!' 'March in a straight line, or you'll stay all day until you can!'

Eventually, in alphabetical order, we lined up in the assembly hall, numbering 500 or so. Half the school was girls, the other half boys, and 'N'er the twain shall meet.' That rule was absolute.

The mood in the hall was quiet, still and utterly depressing. The headmaster, Mr Brown, a medium-sized man with gaunt features and far-away eyes, presided over us from a podium. His second-in-command, Mr Taylor, stood alongside him. These two impressive personalities loomed over us, exuding total authority. In a strange, quiet delivery, Mr Brown introduced the rest of his staff. To his left, stretching down the side of the hall: Mr Outhwaite, Mr Musket, Mr Bedford, Mr Mann and Mr Dalton. Each man's head nodded in turn, acknowledging his name. The roll-call continued on the opposite side: Mr Ogly, Mr Jones, Mr Donaldson, Mr Moran and Mr Hardy. The headmaster continued in his strange, detached voice, 'In this school you will find strict rules. These you will learn from your teachers, and I promise that if you do not adhere to them, you will have me to contend with. Within this framework of rules you will find ample opportunity for an enjoyable education. This school offers a wide range of subjects from English to sport and gardening. You see the large emblem behind me, depicting an eagle flying to the stars? That symbolizes our school motto: "To the uttermost. To the uttermost." That is what I expect from you. Let us pray.' His piercing eyes closed as he intoned the morning prayer, '. . . to labour without asking any reward, saving knowing that we do Thy will, Amen. Now, march in single file to your classrooms. And no talking!'

I found myself in Class 1C – the bottom class – under the watchful eye of Mr Dalton. We were considered somewhat hopeless, and the best that could be expected of us was that we should behave ourselves and possibly learn a few basics. In short, we were the dunce class. Any teacher who found himself in charge of 1C considered himself to be doing some form of penance. Mr Dalton was no exception. He had a stocky frame, thinning hair and tired eyes that viewed us with a kind of weary fatalism.

Except for a few friends from my previous school, there was not a friendly face in sight. My thoughts drifted to the recently departed summer and a splendid holiday at my Uncle George's. Bliss! My eyes closed. I could smell the sweet air and see the low-lying rock pools at Newbiggin, full of pretty fish and multi-coloured crabs.

'What's your name, boy?' growled Mr Dalton, rudely awakening me from my dream.

'Blessed, Sir,' I answered.

'Well, get on with your paper and stop gaping like a moonstruck calf!'

My first impression of our headmaster as a remote and cold man proved quite wrong, however. His watchful eyes and penetrating mind had observed all. A tremendous change was about to take place. He took charge of our class. We were on the edge of our seats, trying valiantly to please him, when he suddenly stood up, smiled mischievously and said, 'I think you need greater help than I can give you; someone of the order of a giant! Do any of you know what a giant is?'

'Yes, Sir,' I spoke out. 'Someone five times bigger than a man.'

'Indeed, Blessed,' he replied. 'But I am thinking of someone even larger than that . . . a complete earth-trembler! In a week's time you will all be confronted by this "giant".'

When the day arrived, we stood with bated breath in the classroom, awaiting the promised titan. Mr Dalton was no longer there, his chair stood empty. The tension was unbearable. Then, gradually, a faint sound grew louder. Light footsteps approached. The door opened and Mr Brown, with a hint of a twinkle in his eye, quietly and proudly announced the name of our new teacher: 'Mrs Brown' he said. Never can jaws have dropped so fast or so low. My God! Women were not supposed to teach here. It was an absolute rule. Where was the promised giant? Not only was this 'giant' a woman, but she was also quite old, in her mid-50s, and very small – no more than 5 feet (1.5 m) tall and with spectacles on the end of her nose. Two woollen cardigans festooned her upper body; large, thick woollen socks ran down into a pair of cushioned slippers.

There was a long silence as the woollen pixie surveyed us. Mr Brown coughed to clear his throat, 'I leave you in good hands . . .' he said, and vanished.

An ominous silence reigned. Then there was a slight movement as she looked down her long nose to get a different angle on us. All the while absolute stillness prevailed.

Then, like a pixie, she did two pirouettes on the spot, drew a deep breath, turned her back on us (a dangerous thing to do) and began to wipe the blackboard clean. We all broke into fits of giggles. Maurice Cook, one of the bolder members of the class, imitated the pixie pirouette, provoking even more suppressed laughter. It is doubtful that in the entire history of warfare, a missile has ever been propelled with such force as the wooden board rubber that hit Cook on the side of the head. The pinpoint accuracy would have impressed even William Tell! In no more than a second, from within the folds of her cardigan, the pixie brandished a small, thin cane, lashing out like lightning on the fists of the half-dozen or so gigglers who had not had time to hide their smirks, or their hands.

Cook, who was holding his ear, shocked, and in pain, found himself bent double as the pixie, with amazing energy and speed, applied a vice-like grip to his other ear and propelled him through the classroom door, straight to the headmaster's study. There, the pixie informed us on her return, his dancing career was receiving great encouragement. There was not a vestige of ill will or temper in her behaviour, just an awe-inspiring demonstration of a discipline that made a deep and lasting impression.

As quickly as it had begun, it stopped. A great silence again filled the room. We all stood like ramrods as she moved her hand across the blackboard, scribbling scores of numbers. Then, stopping abruptly, she aimed the remaining half-inch of chalk at the waste-paper basket and threw it with great accuracy. We ducked our heads, thinking it was for us.

'Einstein.' She spoke quietly. 'Albert Einstein: the greatest living scientist, the creator of the theory of relativity . . . But of course, I am addressing blockheads who are liable to confuse him with Frankenstein!'

We didn't laugh at this.

'You are all known throughout the school as "woodentops", and it is said that that at every turn of your heads you leave a deposit of sawdust . . . is that how you wish to remain?'

'No,' we replied weakly.

'Speak up, I can't hear you.'

'No.' The response was firmer this time.

'Very well,' she grimaced, 'I promise you this: in six months' time you will have a deep love and understanding of the likes of Einstein, and a knowledge and growth that will astound the rest of the school! I will do all in my power to drag you into the light so you can hold your heads up and be proud of yourselves.'

After another pause she requested that we should sit, at the same time nodding to the returning Maurice Cook to take his place.

'This is a maths lesson, I understand . . . normally.' She smiled.

'Let's forget about that. Instead, I'm going to read you a story, *The Hound of the Baskervilles* by Sir Arthur Conan Doyle.'

We were transfixed. She read brilliantly, filling our minds with the haunting mystery and ending with the words, '. . . it was the footprint of the giant hound!'

'Oh, please go on, Mrs Brown,' we begged.

'I will,' she smiled. 'Another day.'

Those 'other days' proved to be wonderful, and school became a place of exciting achievement. Mrs Brown had astonishing drive, determination and an infinite devotion to bringing out our individual gifts. I found myself racing to school, in the knowledge that something new would be revealed to me. Shakespeare, Shaw, Wilde, Masefield, Keats, Wordsworth: she introduced us to them all. When she spoke of the Greeks and their history, we could feel the stones of the Parthenon and the heat of the sun. The wanderings of Odysseus came alive when Mrs Brown recounted his adventures. Tears ran down her cheeks as she described his yearning and loneliness.

For Mrs Brown we worked with integrity and zest, trying our utmost to please her and to meet her high standards. She had a sweet way with incentives, giving presents and prizes of apples and oranges, comics, rare magazines and books on various subjects. I managed to win a prize for English essays three times in a row. This, combined with good reading tests, edged out my fellow competitor, Raymond Finbow (incidentally a marvellous goalkeeper), by two points. For my efforts I won two *Eagle* comics, a stack of copies of *Hotspur* and *Wizard*, and a bag of oranges.

Shortly before the summer holidays of 1948 we learned that Mrs Brown was to leave us. It was revealed that her stay had been intended to be a temporary one, just to put us 'on the right road'. We were devastated. She had become the light of our lives. The dear pixie had led us to the rainbow's end, to the pot of gold. It is no exaggeration to say that she had shown us new frontiers and lifted us to ever-greater heights. As unobtrusively as he had introduced her, Mr Brown gently took her hand, and led her away.

A week later Mr Quemanet was appointed as our teacher. The headmaster had obviously taken a great deal of time in selecting him to fill the gap left by Mrs Brown. He had colossal energy and a fertile imagination. His stocky physique, Continental manner – he would wear shorts some days – and his broad, ready smile made you feel happy and free. Geography, history, drama, art – he invested all the subjects he taught with freshness and a much-appreciated simplicity.

My zest for life and my love and yearning for prehistoric times intrigued him. We got on famously.

My ability to produce a frog or a newt at a moment's notice caused him no end of amusement. Consequently he made me the proud guardian of the natural history unit of the school. I was tickled pink and tirelessly roamed the length and breadth of the Don and Dearne Valley in my quest to find new specimens for the aquariums in the unit. My exploits could be favourably compared with those of the first fairy in *A Midsummer Night's Dream*:

> '*Over hill, over dale,*
> *Thorough bush, thorough brier,*
> *Over park, over pale,*
> *Thorough flood, thorough fire . . .*'
> William Shakespeare, *A Midsummer Night's Dream*, Act II, Scene i

Unfortunately, my adventurous spirit was about to land me into trouble. About a mile from the school was a large stretch of water called the Brick Pond. It was forbidden territory for children. Its sides were steep, way down beneath the surface of the water. There were ledges underneath that could trap you if you fell in. Several people had drowned there and it had taken the police days to find them. My parents were united in spelling out the stern rule that I should 'never, ever, ever go there!'

To me this sinister and dark place was an unexplored continent. There might be untold treasures there and the prospect of visiting this forbidden territory soon became irresistible.

Guilty, yet impelled by the call of the forbidden, I would sometimes venture to this dark water. Contrary to what my parents would have me believe, I discovered that opposite to the dangerous part of the pond was a shallow friendly side that was infested with glorious sticklebacks. A small branch with a length of string and a bent pin knotted to one end made a fine fishing rod! Small, wire worms could easily be scooped from the clay for bait. They were irresistible to the fish. All my captives were then safely transported to the aquariums at the school.

A couple of weeks later something I'd seen at the Brick Pond led to an extraordinary confrontation with several of my teachers. My description of the toads' mating habits provoked an unexpected reaction.

'They're all dead,' I explained. 'I can't understand it. The little male holds on to the female and after they've mated they won't let go. They all gather together in a great big ball, bigger than any football. They choke each other to death.'

This was instantly and arrogantly dismissed. 'Nonsense, Blessed. This is another of your fairy stories.'

The disbelieving teachers loomed over me, pouring scorn on my repeated protestations. The maths teacher was particularly vitriolic.

'The word "pathological", Blessed,' he sneered, 'look it up in a dictionary, lad, because that's what you are rapidly becoming. You live in Cloud-cuckoo-land. You never pay proper attention in class, you fill the heads of other pupils with ridiculous stories of dinosaurs and space monsters. This has got to stop, lad.'

'It's not madness. It's not. It's true,' I insisted. 'I got a big stick and prodded at them, 'cos some of them were still alive; but I couldn't part them. There's thousands of them, all over the pond . . . rotting.'

My story had an immediate impact on scores of the boys. After school a mass exodus took place, all heading for the Brick Pond. There they saw it for themselves and on all sides a chorus of voices burst out, 'He's right.'

'They're all bloody dead!'

'My God!'

'Uuuuuuuuuhhhhhh!'

'They're all rotted.'

The next day they reported their findings to the school, causing general consternation and I basked in my vindication.

The tragic incident of the toads baffled me. Mr Ogly suggested that it was probably a 'mass mating spree' that had simply got out of hand. But this answer didn't satisfy me and I still don't understand it to this day.

There was something sinister about it, as if the toads were under orders to die. They were locked together in at least twenty groups that were larger than footballs. None survived. It was very sad. Their frightful resolve reminded me of the death plunge of the lemmings. Maybe, one day, David Bellamy will write to me and explain it. I would be grateful. I have certainly never witnessed anything like it since, but it only served to increase my interest in the animal kingdom.

3

THE LOST WORLD

In the autumn of that year I was overjoyed to hear that the BBC Light Programme was to broadcast the serial that they had made of Sir Arthur Conan Doyle's *The Lost World*. Unfortunately it was scheduled to be at 1.00 o'clock on Wednesday afternoons for the next ten weeks! This presented me with a dilemma. Each episode ran for 45 minutes, finishing at 1.45 p.m. Afternoon school started at 1.30. If I listened to the entire episode I would be 20 minutes late at least and in such a disciplined school as ours this would not be tolerated.

Of course, the prospect of hearing *The Lost World* proved irresistible. I arranged to listen to it on a wooden radio in a tiny shop called Betty's Penny Bun Shop, which was only about 100 yards (90 m) from the school. Once the episode was over, I ran like the wind and confronted the teachers with some cock-and-bull story about not feeling well. This was accepted for the first couple of weeks, but after that I was for the high jump.

Every pupil at school experienced the cane at least once a term, though at least half the teachers didn't feel compelled to use one. Mr Brown, the headmaster, had a long, thin cane which was in shreds at its end. This made it a deadly instrument of torture and there wasn't a lad in the school who didn't fear it.

When I was late for the third time in a row, I was summoned in front of the entire school on to the podium in the assembly hall. Mr Brown was stunned to see me, as I had been his wife's favourite pupil. Several other lads went before me and were severely caned for various misdemeanours, then it was my turn.

As I turned to look at him I could hear one or two of the other boys crying but I kept my eyes steadfastly on the headmaster. I thought, 'You'll get no change out of me, Mr Brown.' After all, I was respected by the lads for my toughness. I'd been 'Cock' (best fighter) at Highgate Junior School and I therefore had a reputation to keep up.

Slowly he lifted the cane to a great height and brought it down viciously on my right hand. The pain was excruciating but I kept my face straight. Twice more he hit that hand and then administered three more blows to the other.

I walked away as if nothing had happened and then spent twenty minutes in the toilets running my hands under the cold water tap to take the pain away. Imagine the headmaster's surprise when I appeared on the podium the following week for further punishment. Week in and week out I was brought in front of him. It became a ritual. I was just grateful that *The Lost World* was only ten episodes, when it might easily have been twenty!

On the eighth occasion, Mr Brown lifted the cane and then stopped and asked quietly why I was repeatedly late. I was reluctant to tell him because I didn't think that he would understand, and I would probably get more strokes of the cane.

'Come on Blessed,' he hissed, 'why are you constantly late for school on Wednesday afternoons?'

I swallowed hard and then said boldly, 'I listen to *The Lost World*, Sir, on the BBC Light Programme.'

The headmaster said nothing. I swallowed hard again and continued, 'It's being broadcast on the radio, Sir, and 'cos it lasts for three-quarters of an hour, Sir, it runs into school time. I 'ave to listen to it, Sir. Sorry Sir, I just thought it was worth being caned for.'

Mr Brown lowered his arm and stared long and hard at me. After what seemed an eternity he motioned for me to join the rest of the assembly. He quietly uttered the morning prayers, '. . . to labour without asking any reward, save knowing that we do Thy will. Amen.'

Later that day, and much to our surprise, he came to our classroom and politely interrupted the history lesson. Mr Brown asked me to join him and face the class. He spoke gently and said, 'I think it is only right and proper that I should apologize to Blessed for all the canings I have given him over the last few weeks. I was in the wrong. I am also giving you permission, Blessed, to listen to the last two episodes of *The Lost World* without any fear of further punishment. I find the act of caning detestable and I look forward to the day when I am no longer compelled to do it. In the meantime, as a treat, I shall ask Mr Jones to read *The Lost World* to all of you.'

We greeted this news with a terrific cheer for the English teacher, Mr Jones, was a great favourite and a marvellous story-teller. I felt on cloud nine and was so thrilled I could hardly control my emotions. The headmaster concluded by saying, 'I owe a debt of gratitude to Blessed for reminding me what a fine piece of literature *The Lost World* is.'

Wearing a big smile, he strode to the classroom door and was about to leave when he turned suddenly and, with mischief written all over his face said, 'Oh, by the way, this is supposed to be a history lesson. Tell me, where did civilization first begin?'

'In Mesopotamia,' we roared.

'And what is Mesopotamia?' he shouted back.

'The cradle of civilization,' we thundered.

He nodded, smiled and left us triumphant.

The following spring Mr Quemanet suggested that our class should put on a play and present it to the rest of the school.

'Find a tale,' he said, 'And put your own words to it.'

This excited us, but we puzzled over what subject to choose.

'Rumpelstiltskin!' I said. 'That's a right grand tale, that is.'

So Rumpelstiltskin it was.

The two weeks of rehearsal were absolutely terrific, Mr Quemanet urging us on and showing great appreciation of our efforts.

Maurice Cook, known as Mousie to his friends, played the miller's daughter, Billy Platt played the miller and everyone else the villagers. I, of course, played Rumpelstiltskin. To this day I still remember the strange, deep-throated, frog-like voice I used for the part. This, combined with gymnastic leaps and bounds, seemed to work very well.

We performed the play only once, during a lunch hour, and the whole school attended. The headmaster kindly allowed my mother to come (unfortunately, my father was at work) and it was a sweet sight to see her sitting with all the lads in the hall.

Our audience roared approval throughout and seemed to thoroughly enjoy the performance. Afterwards the praise flowed, and Mr Jones, who was to be a major influence in my later years, told my mother that I was a good actor.

The following day, at lunch-time, Mr Donaldson ordered us to stop eating. With one gigantic heave of his body, he surveyed us with his fiery black eyes.

'What happened yesterday in the play?' he demanded.

He targeted poor John Cox, the slowcoach of our class, who offered, 'Blessed was funny, Sir . . .'

After a look of contempt, Mr Donaldson roared dramatically, 'Blessed did something of paramount importance.'

At this stage he was looking directly at me. I was praying that he wouldn't ask me what it was, for I had no idea what he was talking about. He continued, 'When the miller's daughter finally guessed his name, before he began to laugh so wildly, what did Blessed do? . . . He paused! He paused! Pauses are as important as speech is in the art of drama. Anyway, that's what he did, he paused!'

4

HEROES AND MONSTERS

After two years of glorious hot summers and cold, snowy winters, I arrived at the age of 14. For the first time in my life I felt as if I was no longer outside, looking in on an adult world. Entertainment and exploration in particular, had always seemed remote and inaccessible. Now I realized that I did have something special of my own and that I could fulfil my dreams.

Oh! What vistas lay before me. What adventures!

One warm spring night in 1951, I lay down in a field close to my home. There I closed my eyes and could see a mighty river to challenge; a peaceful mountain valley to walk through to a mystical 'Shangri-La'; a massive Himalayan giant to climb; a wondrous tropical rain forest to explore; and a cold frozen fog on the Patagonian ice-cap to penetrate.

When I opened my eyes I saw the vast pool of the nocturnal sky above me. There I was, lying on my back, with outstretched arms, face to face with a hatchery of vibrant coloured stars.

Let me break free, I thought, from Earth's possessive gravity and float to the heavens to discover the many mansions that Jesus spoke of. The whole of the Milky Way seemed to be smiling down on me. God! It must be teeming with life, I thought. I experienced a deep yearning to explore beyond the solar system. It was a feeling of wanting to go to a different home.

The night was still; the silence, breathtaking. I closed my eyes once more and all thoughts disappeared. I sensed a presence and experienced 'the peace that passeth all understanding'.

After half an hour or so of what I suppose was a form of meditation, I opened my eyes and murmured the words of Wordsworth's 'Tintern Abbey':

And I have felt
A presence that disturbs me with the joy
Of elevated thoughts; a sense sublime
Of something far more deeply interfused,
Whose dwelling is the light of setting suns,
And the round ocean and the living air,
And the blue sky, and in the mind of man:
A motion and a spirit, that impels
All thinking things, all objects of all thought,
And rolls through all things.

I stood and looked up at the vast tapestry of the heavens and listened to the stillness of the South Riding of Yorkshire.

A few days later, much to my delight, my dad bought me a fine second-hand bicycle. It was a Raleigh Racer and the same colour as the legendary steam train 'The Flying Scotsman': apple green. This wonderful gift, which he could ill afford, gave me my first taste of independence. No longer was I restricted to the bus routes. Now I had the means to explore the numerous hidden byways of my beloved county.

There is a marvellous moment in the film *The Thief of Baghdad* when the thief uncorks a strange bottle on a lonely beach and a gigantic genie soars out of it and roars, 'Free! Free at last! After 2,000 years.'

That's how I felt. Free as a bird! With my legs pumping ten to the dozen, like the pistons of an express train, my face as red as a beetroot, I raced up hill and down dale in euphoric celebration of my trusty steed. God! I was so proud of that bike. I kept it well oiled and polished and could repair a puncture before you could say 'Bob's Yer Uncle'. My skill as a cyclist grew quickly and I raced round hairpin bends at breakneck speed, and could stop abruptly on a sixpence if I needed to.

'You'll break yer bloody neck, yer daft bugger,' shouted a neighbour, but I took no gorm (notice) of him.

Early one Saturday morning, I decided to cycle to the coast. With my head held low over my racing handlebars, I powered my way through Goldthorpe and headed in the direction of Doncaster. Two miles (5 km) down the road I came to a signpost: Brodsworth to the left, Barnburgh to my right. Barnburgh was famous locally for its 'Cat and Man' church. The story goes that Sir Percival Cresacre, a

Knight Templar, fought a tremendous battle with a wild cat in 1477. The fight was long and bloody. It raged from distant High Melton woods, via Harlington, and ended on the porch of Barnburgh's church, where the mortally wounded knight finally succeeded in crushing the cat. The porch floor was said to be stained with blood which resisted all efforts to scrub it clean.

Though Barnburgh wasn't on my itinerary, I could not resist the appeal of the story, so I turned right and headed in that direction.

The church proved fascinating, but it was the porch floor, stained in ancient blood, that took my breath away.

Oh boy! I thought. What a terrible fight that must have been, and what kind of cat was it? Did the Knight Templars bring animals to Britain from their travels abroad? Was it a leopard, or a tiger, or perhaps a mountain lion? Couldn't have been a Scottish wild cat, they are much too small!

I mounted my bike and quickly rejoined the road to the east. My mind was a maelstrom of dark, bloody images. Mile after mile I rode onward, soaked in sweat. I find that rhythm stimulates my imagination and so in unison with the motion of the wheels of my bike, my thoughts raced round and round. From the bloodstained porch at Barnburgh my mind leapt to the even bloodier hall at Heoriot in medieval times. There in that Anglo-Saxon castle, the great Scandinavian hero Beowulf fought a titanic battle with the awesome monster Grendal. Sir Percival Cresacre's struggle with the cat made me think of Beowulf's ordeal. I chewed over a wild conversation that I had with my English teacher, Mr Jones. It was he, with his mischievous brown eyes, dark wavy hair, handsome looks and bright resonant voice, who first introduced me to the epic Anglo-Saxon poem *Beowulf*. The prehistoric hero of my childhood, Strang the Terrible, was now consigned to a warm but tiny room at the very back of my mind, and the shining armoured Saxon knight had taken his place.

Mr Jones and I had debated the saga at some length.

'What was the reason for Grendal's appalling behaviour?' I asked him out of the blue one day.

'What do I say about that? I say, Blessed, that you are growing up by the minute. But to answer your questions, I can do no other than read from 'Beowulf' itself and leave it to you to come to your own conclusions.'

He found the appropriate page and in his beautiful baritone, read the famous lines that are etched in my memory:

'The grim spirit was called Grendal, the renowned traverser of the marches, who held the moors, the fen and fastness; unblessed creature, he dwelt for a while in the lair of monsters after the creator had condemned them. On Cain's kindred did the everlasting Lord avenge the murder, for that he had slain Abel; he had no joy of that feud, but the creator drove him afar from mankind for that misdeed.

Thence all evil broods were born, ogres and elves and evil spirits – the giants also, who for a long time fought with God, for which he gave them their reward.'

Mr Jones closed the book, looked at me intensely and quietly said, 'You see, Blessed, Grendal and his awesome mother, with whom he lived in the underwater cave, are no longer really part of the community of men. They are inextricably linked with the first blood-carnage of Cain. They are exiles, outcasts, and are utterly condemned.'

'It seems a bit harsh, Sir,' I said.

'Yes indeed, Blessed,' he replied. 'But here is an extract from St Augustine's *The City of God*, which might clarify things for you. Augustine acknowledges, in respect of Genesis 6:1–4, that there were indeed such creatures as giants. It says,

And it pleased the Creator to produce them, that it might thus be demonstrated that neither beauty, nor yet size and strength are of such moment to the wise men, whose blessedness lies in spiritual and immortal blessings, in far better and more enduring gifts, in the good things that are the peculiar property of the good, and are not shared by good and bad alike.

'It is this that another prophet confirms when he says, "These were the giants, famous from the beginning, that were of so great stature, and so expert in war. Those did NOT the Lord choose, neither gave he the way of knowledge unto them; but they were destroyed because they had no wisdom, and perished through their own foolishness."'

Three hours later, with St Augustine's words still pulsating in my brain, I arrived on the seafront at Bridlington.

It was mid-afternoon and the tide was in. The sky was overcast and the wind was bitter. I put on my balaclava and thick jersey to keep the cold out and bought a fish and three pennyworth of chips from the nearest fish and chip shop. I settled down on a wooden bench on the promenade, tucked into my grub and feasted my eyes on the vast expanse of the North Sea.

Across that stretch of water, I thought, is the land where Beowulf is purported to have lived. 'Beowulf! Beowulf!' I murmured to myself. Did he really exist? What kind of strength did he possess to tear off Grendal's gigantic metallic claw? What terror must have been in the monster's heart when it felt the power of Beowulf's arm! What agony the creature must have been in as it slowly made its way back to its lair to die in Sycarax's arms!

My macabre thoughts started to make me laugh. It was ridiculous! I ask you. There I was, with my belly full of fish and chips, sitting on a bench in quaint Bridlington, with my head full of images of giants and monsters.

Yet I couldn't shake off the allure of the legendary tale. My mind hummed with Beowulf's adventures, and with the image of the fearsome Grendal.

When I was 14 years old my father was injured very badly in a roof fall at Hickleton Main Colliery.

My mother pointed out ruefully that I was a big lad, with a large appetite and that she couldn't possibly make ends meet on my father's small sick pay, so I would have to leave school and go to work. My father's injuries were serious, though he made a marvellous recovery after about 18 months of intensive treatment at a rehabilitation centre in nearby Pirbeck. But it was too late to save my education.

Leaving my beloved school made me sick with unhappiness. I had been a late developer but now I was galloping along at a pace and doing really well. I was to have been made School Captain and I was favourite to win the 880 and the 440 yards at the Don Valley inter-school games! But there was nothing to be done about it. I felt sick and downcast but quite simply, I had to do my best to help with the family budget.

It was by no means easy to find work so to start I got a job as an undertaker's assistant earning £1.15 shillings a week. This was followed by a better paid job, £2.10 shillings a week as a plasterer's apprentice on the local building sites. Throughout this period I was helped by some of my old teachers from school, who very kindly gave me tuition three nights a week and on alternate weekends. I also made myself a member of a prestigious amateur dramatic society called the Mexborough Theatre Guild. The standard of this excellent society rivalled the fine professional repertory company in nearby Sheffield.

Mum and Dad in 1937 with me, aged one.

'Watch the dinosaur!' Me aged six.

In the school production of *The Wise Men of Gotham (top row, second from left)*.

Strang the Terrible.

All that remains of Goldthorpe
Picture House, the centre of our
universe, where I saw *King Kong*
and *Flash Gordon*.

The pond where I saw the dying toads.

Tomb of Sir Percival Cresacre, 1477 AD, the knight in the 'Cat and Man' legend.

Sir Arthur
Conan Doyle,
author of *The
Lost World*.

As Long John Silver, the day after my encounter with crocodiles in Jamaica.

The American crocodile, as seen by me at the crocodile farm in Jamaica.

The crocodile is one of nature's greatest success stories, spanning 160 million years. A living dinosaur! *Top:* Nile crocodile, *bottom:* American crocodile.

A frendly kiss from my wife Hildegard and daughter Rosalind before departing for Aconcagua.

With Steve Bell before the climb.

Aconcagua, the Stone Sentinel, the highest mountain in the western hemisphere.

Puente del Inca, the jumping-off point for Aconcagua.

Back at base camp after carrying supplies up the mountain.

At 16,000 feet in my 'Babygro'.

Me *(on the left)* with the redoubtable and happy John Knowles at 17,000 feet.

At 20,000 feet with the mighty Andes in the background.

Standing near the dead German climber we saw in the snow. He looked for all the world like one of those chocolate soldiers that my mother used to hang on the Christmas tree.

Leading at 22,000 feet. This picture gives no indication of the strong winds of up to 80 mph which battered us as we climbed.

Having gone through blood, snot and diarrhoea, I finally reach the summit of Aconcagua.

The successful summit team on the roof of the Stone Sentinel.

The entire Roraima expedition group at Mochima. *Standing from left:* Janet Butterworth, Andrew Bawn, David Gardiner, Nick Moss, me, Silva, Karen Pearce, Tim Pearce and Cortez. *Kneeling:* Miles Butterworth and Maz Moss.

The beautiful sandy beaches of an island paradise off Mochima where we rested and acclimatised before the expedition.

Maz reading *The Lost World* in Mochima.

With Maz, Mochima.

Mad dogs and Englishmen jump in the sea
in the midday sun, Mochima.

Filming with my faithful camera, Mochima.

Kama Falls in the Gran Sabana.

Kamaracoto children at the camp site.

Gran Sabana campsite.

Anthony Rivas with the faithful Babeto weighing and distributing supplies for the porters at Perai Tepui.

Campsite at Perai Tepui.

The leader of the Kamaracoto porters who helped us on our climb.

Turkey vultures at Kamarata.

One of the beautiful flowers of the Gran Sabana.

The Guild was run by a very gifted man called Harry Dobson. This titanic man, stormed, bullied, cajoled and dragged me into the light. I was also blessed with a first-rate speech teacher from Rotherham, called Frank Cooper and an eccentric but divine drama teacher from Hoyland called Ruth Wyn Owen. Miss Owen also taught Patrick Stewart, now of *Star Trek* fame. This fine triumvirate, backed by my parents, saved my life.

An enthusiastic area youth adviser by the name of Fred Lawson frequently popped in to offer guidance. The Chief Education Officer of Yorkshire, a certain Mr Hyles, focused his eyes in my direction and an awesome intellectual called Gerald Tyler, the drama adviser of South Yorkshire, nodded approvingly at my progress. I was lucky! With such help, the disappointment of leaving school finally disappeared. When I had completed my National Service I was almost 20 years old and I was astonished to receive a full drama scholarship from the Yorkshire Education Authority in Wakefield to go to the much celebrated Bristol Old Vic Theatre School. Now I was on cloud nine. It was unheard of, for a coal-miners son to go to drama school. My mum and dad were dead chuffed about it.

I celebrated a couple of weeks later by setting out on my first solo 'mountaineering' expedition, to climb the modest hill, Mam Tor in Derbyshire, but fled terrified, when a black cloud enveloped me near the summit!

'Your acting career may be progressing in leaps and bounds,' said Dad, 'but yer not much cop as an explorer. And you want to climb Mount Everest and go to the Lost World, but you can't even get up Mam Tor! I could climb the bugger backwards!'

One Saturday my father and I climbed the disused railway embankment at the back of our house together.

As we walked I told him once again, that though I was dedicated to acting there was a part of my being that ached to be an explorer.

'You see, Dad, as the poet says, "Acting is holding a mirror up to life." Whereas exploring this magnificent planet, is life. But don't worry, I'm not about to climb some great mountain, or wrestle with bone-crunching anacondas in the Lost World just yet, but I will find space for it in my life one day; otherwise I will feel incomplete and unhappy.'

Dad smiled and gently threw an affectionate punch. 'In a few days, Brian lad, you will be leaving home to go to the Bristol Old Vic Theatre School. It goes without saying that we are all going to miss you, particularly yer mother. Yer won't forget to come home when yer can lad, and yer won't forget Yorkshire, will yer?'

'What are you talking about, Dad?' I responded. 'Forget home and York-shire? They are in my heart forever.'

But though I had impressed on my father my total love of Yorkshire I still felt in my heart of hearts a deep yearning to see and breathe in the dense syrupy air of ancient Pangea. Oh! I thought, if only science could invent the Time Machine of H. G. Wells, so that I could go back to that ancient continent and allow my curious senses to take in the wonders of the primeval landscape, for then I would see an amazing diversity of life and massive forests of conifers, ginkgo, and giant tree-ferns.

The day before I was to leave home, I went upstairs to check that I had packed everything.

My bedroom-cum-sitting room was a square box. The walls were completely bare, and yet within the confines of these walls my imagination had run riot.

My pride and joy was a second-hand Bush gramophone, and over the years I had painstakingly acquired a fine collection of records. There were books everywhere – even cramming the drawers of my large, yellow dresser – ranging from Shakespeare to every conceivable tome on adventure, daring tales such as the exploits of Mallory and Irvine on Everest and Thor Heyerdahl's voyage on the Kon-Tiki.

In my imagination I journeyed with these intrepid explorers. Brimming with pride, I accompanied the renowned Baron Von Humbolt in Ecuador as he attempted to climb the mighty Chimborazo, and then shared his anguish as he ultimately failed. I sailed with him as he bade farewell to that continent just as the majestic volcano, Cotopaxi, erupted, as if in celebration of his astonishing achievements.

The deeds of the explorers leapt off the pages, their bodies materialized on my bed and enacted their adventures before my very eyes. My brain would then seize up from too much excitement, and at the snap of my book my visitors would reluctantly flee.

My window also looked out into a world of wonders. Of all the places on God's Earth, I doubt if any room received the afternoon sun quite like mine. Some days it glared, chillingly white, and at other times it smouldered, a warm red. No two sunsets were the same.

That evening, as altocumulus clouds appeared to be static around the flaming orb and its rays penetrated every corner of the pink sky, I pressed the button of my gramophone, watched the needle find the first groove, and crept back to the window. With the setting sun pouring golden light into my room, I waited breathlessly. Gradually and almost imperceptibly the sounds of Ravel's 'Daphnis and Chloe' filtered through the air. The haunting sounds kissed the deepest reaches of my brain and carried me off to far-distant lands.

Over the moors I went, heading south-west, past magical Tintagel, then west across the grey, stormy Atlantic until, plunging and driving on, I could make out the undulating eastern seaboard of the USA. As it tantalizingly revealed itself, I followed its jagged contour until the fresh breeze whistled up the warmth of the south. Then, as I skirted fast and low around the Gulf of Mexico, my senses quickened with the promise of Conan Doyle's Maple White Land.

Up, up, high above black nimbus, I soared towards a cyclopean landscape of fiery volcanoes. Before the cloak of night enveloped me I peered down, down into the cone of the already sleeping Cotopaxi, until its powerful currents tore me away to the confines of the ever-watchful Chimborazo. I hovered here in the blackest night, in darkest Ecuador, a Yorkshire condor humming the hymn, 'Chimborazo, Cotopaxi, took me by the hand'. Surrendering to faith, I floated and soared on jetstreams of joy and alighted, at dawn, on the emerald canopy of the Matto Grosso.

Oh, Brazil! Oh, Venezuela! Oh, dawn of delight! Green, green mansions and a haven of long-lost temples. A never-ending carpet of trees, broken only by the cascading water and ethereal mist of the Angel Falls. Jaguar, ocelot, margay, jaguarundi and our rare friend the kod-kod: all growling, hissing and moving back from the honk-honk of the greedy anaconda. The hum of life! I swooned as my senses, dizzy with delight, sizzled with ecstasy among the flowering aromas. Pollinating powder-puffs leapt out from the stems and dense clouds of morpho butterflies rose in the morning light, their electric-blue wings incandescently reflecting the sun's rays.

The cacophony of sounds rose up – the jungle was alive with celebration.

When 'Daphnis and Chloe' came to an end, I turned off the gramophone and lovingly returned the record to the rack. I lay on the bed and closed my eyes. Gradually the sounds of the Matto Grosso and the jungle faded and I slept.

PART TWO

IN SEARCH OF ADVENTURE

5

DANGEROUS PURSUITS

*Will no one explore Roraima and bring back to us the tidings which it
has been waiting these thousands of years to give us? One of the great
marvels of the mysteries of the Earth lies on the outskirts of one of our
colonies – British Guiana – and we leave the mystery unsolved, the
marvel uncared for!*

The Spectator (1874)

*We were within seven miles from an enormous line of ruddy cliffs
which encircled, beyond all doubt, the plateau of which Professor
Challenger spoke!*

Sir Arthur Conan Doyle, *The Lost World*

From 1956, when I first went to drama school right up to the present day
I have been fortunate to have done lots of theatre, masses of television and many
films. I've been a lucky lad! The gods have been kind to me. I have also had the
good fortune to marry the lovely actress Hildegard Neil, and we have a darling
daughter called Rosalind.

Our home is a cottage near Bagshot in Surrey surrounded by about 3 acres
(1.2 hectares) of land, comprising paddocks, lawns, shrubs and a tiny wood. Within
this idyll we have scores of different farmyard ducks including Aylesburies, Khaki
Cambells, Muscovies, Indian Shellducks, Black Cayugas, Indian Runners,
Mandarins and very raucous Call-ducks, plus all manner of passing mallards and
herons. The barn, stables and paddocks are full of them. They are delightful
company. We have hens strutting their stuff, plus the more usual ponies, dogs, cats

and hundred of moles! Oh, I am forgetting, I also have a 10,000-gallon pond stocked with a fine collection of koi carp.

With great cunning I have managed, over the last 40 years, to pursue my quest for adventure and explore many strange territories. Whenever I have been offered a film in some distant land I have always located the nearest mountain with a view to climbing it. Fortunately, the producers and directors of these films have been unaware of these exploits, or they would probably never have employed me. Actors are always restricted by contract when filming from practising any dangerous pursuits – skating, horse-riding and so on, let alone mountaineering. On one occasion I did come unstuck whilst making a film in Austria in 1969 called *The Last Valley* which starred Michael Caine and Omar Sharif.

When you are making a film abroad, your contract stipulates that when you have completed your last day of filming, you are required to stay within the environs of your hotel for a couple of days until the laboratory developing the film can OK its condition and give you the thumbs up to go home.

So far everything had gone smoothly on this movie and the technicians were as happy as sand boys. So, after completing my part, I decided to chance my arm and 'do a bunk'!

I was so impatient to get to grips with the peaks around Innsbruck that I set off like a demented gorilla and disappeared into the morning mist. Big mistake! Because whilst yours truly was clawing his way up a mountain called Hafelekar, the director, James Clavell, decided that he wanted to reshoot a scene that involved me. Of course I was nowhere to be found. The poor second assistant on the film had hell locating me and he actually had to send several mountain guides to look for me.

'Mr Blessed,' they shouted on their loud hailers, 'you are needed back on the film.'

They eventually managed to locate me high up on a great mountain called 'the Zugspitze'.

You can image how mortified I was as I arrived back on location to encounter the film crew, 500 extras and 60 or 70 actors who represented warriors in the Thirty Years War in the 1600s. In front of them stood Mr Clavell, a big man with strong features who was famous for having written the novel *Shogun*. Although he and I had always gotten on famously, I did feel that I was for the high jump this time.

But not so. Much to my surprise, Clavell greeted me with a broad smile and said, 'Blessed Brian, you mad crazy bastard, you have cost me thousands of pounds and have made me bankrupt! And for that I am going to have you killed.'

His words brought a great cheer from the actors present. I rounded on them in mock defiance, 'You great wassocks! You couldn't hurt a pussy!'

More cheering from the actors and then, speaking between bouts of laughter, Clavell added, 'Mr Blessed, Sir, I am going to do you a great favour, yes I am going to have you killed, and I promise you there is nothing better than a glorious death to start your film career.'

Twenty minutes later I was dressed and ready for action. The character I was playing was called Korski and he was an out-and-out baddie, who exploded on to the scene and killed everyone in sight. My costume was of black leather with silver studs, which had once been worn by that brooding star Jack Palance when he played Attila the Hun. With my rather large arms, cropped hair, short beard and large black mace, I looked exceedingly fearful.

'Action,' said the director. Michael Caine plunged his spike helmet into my stomach and I fell backwards in slow motion, like one of Fred Dibnah's chimneys, into a pig sty full of you know what. As the director said 'Cut' I found myself looking into the face of a small pig, who gave me an affectionate lick. He knew a 'good ham' when he saw one!

After this experience I didn't leave the vicinity of the hotel until the lab technicians had given me definitive clearance.

If you think I had learned my lesson, you are mistaken. Two years later I was up to my old tricks again.

In the spring of 1971 I found myself in Italy, playing the part of Pedro in the musical film *Man of La Mancha*, starring Peter O'Toole and Sophia Loren. The film took several months to make but it gave me the opportunity to explore the wonderful Ibruzzi Mountains. It also brought together a host of actors from England. We were located in Rome and during this time I visited Pompeii and like most visitors ascended Vesuvius. Sicily, too, was tantalizingly close, with its great volcano, Mount Etna. My determination to go these was absolute. The whole area was alive with seismic activity and every square mile is steeped in legend. Stromboli is thought to be the 'fire island' that features in the wanderings of Odysseus. All along the fault line there is volcanic activity on the islands of Lipari and Vulcano; Vulcano being a hot, small steaming island where springs of warm water burst from hidden cracks to form gorgeous, stimulating pools to bathe in. The fault line then leads to Etna, where, beneath the mountain the giant Encladeus sleeps, a Titan who, whenever he changes position, causes an eruption.

During coffee breaks on the set the actors would love to listen to me rattling on about these wonders. Several of them wanted to join me in my exploits. Oh dear! I thought, shades of Innsbruck! Dangerous pursuits were again, of course, strictly *verboten* by contract. Oh well, what the hell! As they didn't give a damn – neither did I.

And so, regardless of the risks, we made several treks into the Ibruzzi, ascending, by easy scramble routes, as many peaks as we could. Of course, I took every precaution with my novice charges and carried lots of gear, which included a rope in perfect condition; I had seen too many people come a cropper with frayed ropes.

One of our party was a fine American pianist and composer, called Larry Rosenthal. Larry was 45 years old at the time, of medium height, slightly balding with strong, sensitive, dark eyes, and an artist to his fingertips. Larry said he wanted to accompany me to Sicily, when I went to climb Mount Etna. The signs were good. The film was to break for a five-day holiday at Easter and planes flew regularly to Catania, taking only three-quarters of an hour to get there. So a few days later, we boarded an aircraft to Sicily and set off on our little expedition.

The plane made a spectacular circle around Etna, veering close to its sides. In the fading light the mountain was dark and sinister with a surprising amount of snow and ice on its flanks. Periodically, in weird contrast, tongues of fire shot out from red fumaroles on the strange, twisted summit cone.

After landing at Catania airport we took a taxi to the Sapienza Refuge at 6,000 feet (1,100 m). I understand that it now no longer exists having been swept away during a major eruption, in which the summit cone was totally destroyed.

At 3.00 o'clock the next morning, suitably dressed and with a 70-foot (21 m) rope tied securely around Larry, I led the way up the ancient lava to the mighty Mount Etna.

We progressed steadily and at 7,000 feet (2,133 m) the dawn broke and filled us with a feeling of well-being and anticipation. The black landscape became multicoloured as the sun's rays moved dramatically and rapidly uphill revealing the mountain's secrets. A vast panorama of snow-fields, ridges, gullies and smoking hot vents all pointed the way to the pyramid and final summit cone. The last obstacle was dark and sinister.

For a while the vista looked like a scene from Dante's *Inferno*; that is, until the full power of the sun embraced it. With arms around each other's shoulders, Larry and I watched the sunrise. The wonderful golden orb gave its warmth and light to every nook and cranny of the volcano, banishing its former quality and transforming it to a thing of haunting beauty. Nothing was said, all was silent and still.

Our progress took up to 10,000 feet (3,048 m). Our excitement knew no bounds. We could discern the curvature of the Earth. The width at the base of the volcano is 89 miles (143 km) and we could feel its roots reaching powerfully through the countryside, influencing all. Oh yes, there was no doubt that the mighty Titan, Encladeus, resided under it!

Be still, Giant, I thought, no eruption today! After all, I had been informed that on occasions, when the fellow did awaken, resulting lava flows from the side vents could exceed 60 mph (96 kph). This was a piece of information that I did not reveal to my gallant companion.

Etna is almost 11,000 feet (3,353 m) high and the final pyramid at that time had a 60-degree slope which had both of us panting. On finally arriving at the summit we embraced in triumph, then tried to find a cool place to sit down. This proved nigh on impossible as each resting pace was so hot it singed our trousers.

We explored the lip of the main crater and several small caldera that led from it. I manipulated myself into a safe position from where I could peer down into the cauldron, with a handkerchief protecting my nose and mouth. I was stunned by the sight that greeted me 100 feet (30 m) below. A small lake of lava gently rose and fell, as if breathing to some ancient tune. Periodically, and within seconds its surface appeared to cool and develop a skin streaked with blue veins that formed a tapestry of subtle shapes. Then, in an instant, it would be destroyed again by the consuming fires of the hotter lava down below.

That's what the Earth looked like three thousand million years ago, I thought. All life started in this primordial way. My face began to feel the heat and I hastily, but regretfully, pulled back from this awesome work of nature and wondered if I would ever see its like again.

We looked around us at the primitive landscape, ate our chocolate and slowly drank our coffee, unable to say a word. We experienced an atavistic feeling that the cauldron of overwhelming heat, containing that dreadful vortex of boiling molten lava was, nevertheless, not alien to the chemistry of our own bodies, instead it gave us a strange feeling of belonging, as if there was nothing to fear.

Without a doubt, to climb this wondrous giant volcano, the largest in Europe, was a deep and unique experience. I was so happy for Larry as, for him, the effort was like going to the moon. His face positively glowed with pride and satisfaction. Arriving back at the Sapienza Refuge at 4.00 p.m., we decided to sleep for a few hours, then have dinner and set off for Rome the following morning. Our meal that evening was quiet and reflective. A fire filled the room with its cheer and warmth and the flames highlighted the faces of the two friends contentedly drinking red wine – the red wine from the vines growing in the black soil of Mount Etna, *Lachryma Christi* (The Tears of Christ).

Three days later we were both back at work at the Dino di Laurentis studio in Rome. During a coffee break, Sofia Loren good-naturedly tweaked my nose and said, 'You really are crazy Brian, taking Larry all over the Ibruzzi Mountains and now up Mount Etna. It's all right for you, but he's not used to such strenuous activity, and he might have had a heart attack. Also, he is a great pianist and you could easily have damaged his fingers.'

She then tenderly cupped his face in her delicate hands, muttering 'Poor Larry', and planted a sweet kiss on his blushing cheek, which of course he greatly enjoyed. After all it's not every day that you receive a kiss from Sofia Loren! But she did have a point. It had never entered my thick skull that by taking him rock climbing I had put undue stress on his sensitive fingers. Two weeks later it was announced on TV and radio that Larry was to give a grand solo concert in the eternal city. On the appointed day a large expectant audience of 2,000 or more filled the concert hall to overflowing. Never had I experienced such fear for a fellow artist!

Larry made his entrance, smartly dressed in an evening suit, but his face looked haggard and pale. I shrank into my chair, consumed with nerves. The auditorium lights dimmed, the applause died down, my fists bit into the sides of my cushioned chair and I held my breath. I might as well have spared myself the pain; his fingers hit the piano keys with stunning power, as if his life depended on it. The strength and certainty of his playing electrified the audience. I relaxed as he swept on in triumph. The audience rose as one and bellowed their lungs out in appreciation. In the mayhem that followed, I spirited myself away, scuttling like a demented crab through the dark streets, seeking their cloaking darkness. I was completely overwhelmed with guilt.

Having put a suitable distance between me and the concert hall, I found myself sitting in the gutter, staring out into the hot, humid Roman night. After an hour or so, I felt a hand on my shoulder. Much to my surprise I found Larry's concerned, sensitive face smiling down at me.

'Brian . . . Brian . . . are you all right? What are you doing here? I have been looking for you everywhere. Didn't you like the concert?'

For the next twenty minutes I tried to explain to him that I was overcome by his performance and that I was utterly ashamed that I had so irresponsibly taken him climbing. 'I had no idea, Larry,' I choked, 'that you could play like that. Never in a million years would I have taken you rock climbing had I known.'

Larry put an arm round me, saying, 'Brian, dear Brian. Climbing Mount Etna is arguably the finest achievement of my life. I can never thank you enough for taking me. You wouldn't want me to have missed it, would you?'

He then rubbed my head and continued, 'Come on, let's go to the Trevi Fountain and have a hot chocolate.'

Looking back on this colourful adventure, Larry's claims that the ascent of Etna possibly surpassed anything he had artistically experienced reminded me of an incident in the life of the great Baron von Humboldt.

As you may know, this astonishing man achieved in one immensely long lifetime probably more than any other explorer in history. In a life of 90 years, stretching from the age of Voltaire before the French Revolution until after the publication of Marx's manifesto, he travelled, chronicled, recorded, investigated and discovered so much about this planet that, to this day, more than 2,000 places – mountains, rivers, canyons, ocean currents, even a crater on the moon – bear his name. In 1858, at the age of 89, Humboldt, white-bearded, and now the grand old man of European science, posed reluctantly for a painter in a Berlin studio. When asked what he would like as a background he replied, 'Place me in front of Chimborazo.'

Of all his achievements, it was his failed attempt to climb this 20,000-foot (6,096 m) volcano in Ecuador that remained uppermost in his heart and mind.

6

CROCODILES AND CUTLASSES

Over the next 16 years I had exciting seasons in the Alps, climbing such mountains as the Matterhorn and Mont Blanc. My adventures also took me to various parts of Africa and Asia, and in 1987 I ended up in Jamaica with one leg. But the domain of the Lost World still eluded me.

Of course, I didn't really lose a leg. I am referring to the fact that I played the part of Long John Silver in a Walt Disney/HTV television serial called *Return to Treasure Island*. It was a great script with thousands of extras and wonderful locations in Spain and Jamaica. I can remember standing on the deck of the *Hispaniola* surrounded by my fellow 'shipmates', with the skull and crossbones fluttering in the warm afternoon breeze, and staring at the wide expanse of the Caribbean Sea. Not far across that blissful emerald ocean was South America. Oh! It was so tantalizingly close! God! I felt so frustrated, I longed to go there. I kept squeezing my fists together and whispering emphatically to myself and the universe at large, 'Be patient, Brian, you will get there one day, be patient! Soon! Soon!'

I closed my eyes and hummed the opening tune of Ariel Ramirez's 'Misa Criolla'. As the mood took hold of me, I whistled the blissful 'Navidad En Verano' and the haunting 'Navidad Nuestra'. Standing there motionless, like a bewitched Ulysses, I felt the distant siren call from within the green mansions of Venezuela. Am I in truth an immigrant who has not yet found his homeland? In this delicate state of ecstasy I muttered the words of Deuteronomy 8:7:

> *'For the lord thy God bringeth thee into a good land: a land of brooks*
> *of water, of fountains, and depths that spring out of valleys and hills.'*

I was almost tempted at this point to shout, 'Hoist the sails me hearties, and set out bearings for Venezuela. There's gold there lads! Aye, gold! El Dorado! Bestir yerselves, you landlubbers! I'll show you diamonds and rubies as big as yer fists! Aye, my lucky lads! Sail the Caribbean with Long John Silver and I'll make you as rich as kings.'

I tell you this, ladies and gentlemen, we could have done it too, for we were a first-rate crew and were capable of sailing our marvellous clipper anywhere. After all, did not Sir Walter Raleigh himself show us the way when he sailed to Venezuela in 1594? This famous explorer, historian, soldier, poet and man of letters sacrificed his fortune and life in search of a rich American civilization, whose discovery would enrich England, just as the Incan and Aztec conquests had enriched her Spanish enemies. It was this remarkable man who first sighted and described the Lost World of Roraima. He wrote as follows:

> *I was informed of the Mountain of Christall, to which in trueth for the length of the way, and the evil season of the yeare, I was not able to march, nor abide any longer upon the journey. We saw it farre off and it appeared like a white church towre of exceeding height. There falleth over it a mightie river which toucheth no part of the side of the mountaine, but rusheth over the top of it, and falleth to the ground with a terrible noyse and clamor, as if a thousand great belles were knockt one against another. I think there is not in the world so strange an overfall, not so wonderful to behold. Berreo told me it hath diamonds and other precious stones on it, and that they shined very farre off. But what it hath I knowe not, neither durst he or any of his men ascende to the toppe of the saide mountaine, those people and adjoyning beeing his enemies and the way to it so impassible.*
>
> *Sir Walter Raleigh's Historical Account*

I loved playing the part of Long John Silver. I loved his passion for adventure. It was a passion I could relate to, for I truly believe that the greatest danger in life, is to not take the adventure.

Piers Haggard, the director, was raw-boned and broad-shouldered. He loved swimming and was exceedingly fit. I may have imagined it but I always felt that there was a touch of sadness about him. It was particularly evident one evening during filming. As we gazed up at the heavens, the sadness seemed to pervade the serenity around us.

For a long period of time we just sat and stared. Eventually I broke the silence with gentle enquiries about this sadness. But he evaded my questions and countered with questions about the Royal Shakespeare Company, for whom I had been working for the last two years. But under the Jamaican skies, Stratford did not whet my appetite as a conversational topic and I started to whack on about Venezuela and the Lost World, instead.

Piers sat bolt upright and told me of his life-long ambition to make a film or TV series of Sir Arthur Conan Doyle's novel. I was flabbergasted! A fellow worshipper at last!

Piers exploded around the quarter deck, alighting from time to time on the odd chair, as he spoke with the intensity of this ambition.

'Got to do it, Brian, got to do it,' he said.

'I love the book! It's brilliantly written. All of the characters are fascinating. The whole yarn is so wonderfully real. It goes without saying, Brian, that you were born to play Professor Challenger. I want to be faithful to the book, and film it exactly as Conan Doyle wrote it.'

'I couldn't agree more,' I shouted, jumping up and down in delight. 'Not like that bloody dreadful film they made in 1957. God! They did Conan Doyle an injustice.'

When Doyle wrote his scientific romance *The Lost World*, he put a verse of poetry at the beginning:

> *I have wrought my simple plan*
> *If I give one hour of joy*
> *To the boy who's half a man*
> *Or the man who's half a boy.*

Well, Sir Arthur, all I can say is your simple plan had the desired effect on the two men aboard the *Hispaniola*, in the port of Ocho Rias in July 1987. For the next two hours it was like a tennis match. We tossed ideas back and forth like two eternal Peter Pans.

'We could film most of it in Venezuela,' I said.

'Really?' said Piers.

'Of course,' I replied. 'We could film the actors in the exact locations in the

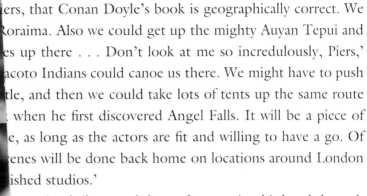

ers, that Conan Doyle's book is geographically correct. We
Roraima. Also we could get up the mighty Auyan Tepui and
es up there . . . Don't look at me so incredulously, Piers,'
acoto Indians could canoe us there. We might have to push
tle, and then we could take lots of tents up the same route
when he first discovered Angel Falls. It will be a piece of
e, as long as the actors are fit and willing to have a go. Of
enes will be done back home on locations around London
ished studios.'

remained silent, and then, after running his hand through
said, 'Right, we'll bloody well do it. Whilst we're at it we'll
other novel, *The Poison Belt*, which features Challenger and
om *The Lost World*.'

shook hands on the deal. Happy as sandboys we sat back
chairs and stared up at the night sky. Some lines from
Tennyson came to me:

es: the slow moon climbs: the deep
many voices. Come my friend,
seek a newer world.
g well in order smite
ows; for our purpose holds
sunset, and the baths
Of all the western stars, until I die.
It may be that the gulfs will wash us down:
It may be we shall touch the Happy Isles,
And see the great Achilles, whom we knew.
Tho' much is taken, much abides; and tho'
We are not now that strength which in old days
Moved earth and heaven; that which we are, we are;
One equal temper of heroic hearts,
Made weak by time and fate, but strong in will
To strive, to seek, to find, and not to yield.

I noticed that the bright moon that had dominated the night sky was now
covered in a thin film of grey cloud, and so the Milky Way could now shine brightly

and display its glittering array of vibrant stars. Much to my amusement, I discovered that the Plough, which points the way to the North Star, was upside-down.

'It's upside-down, Piers,' I said.

'Yes, of course,' replied Piers. 'It always is, in Jamaica.'

And if that sounds like Double Dutch, it isn't. And if Piers and I were happy, we were.

While shooting *Return to Treasure Island* I got the chance to visit a crocodile farm. It was a stunt dreamed up by the production's Publicity Department, though for the life of me I couldn't understand what Long John Silver had to do with crocodiles. Still, the Publicity Department thought it was a great idea and who was I to question their wisdom?

The whole prospect really excited me. I had always been fascinated by crocodiles for they give one a real glimpse into the prehistoric world.

I imparted this opinion to Alf, a stuntman I had become friends with, as we travelled with the photographer in a large press van. His nerve was visibly failing as I described the characteristics of my favourite reptile.

'The cold, hooded gaze of these fearless hunting machines has inspired terror in the human race from the dawn of our history. But, don't forget, Alf dear, that you are supposed to protect me!'

'Don't worry,' he replied, 'I'll be right behind you!'

I laughed and said, 'You know, Alf, the crocodile can be very gentle, almost sensuous with its mate and its young.'

'Well, I don't want any of them kissing me,' he grinned.

'You never know, Alf, you might like it. Romantic, that's what they are! They are truly amazing creatures. Listen to Professor Blessed and learn something. Crocodiles are members of an order of reptiles consisting of alligators, the gharial and the true crocodiles. They are the last survivors of the great group of 'ruling reptiles', the archosaurs. Among their extinct relatives, the best known are the dinosaurs, all descended from common ancestors, the thecodonts, which flourished during the early Tirassic period, 225 million years ago. The fossil records show that modern crocodiles have changed very little since they first appeared about 160 million years ago.

'They are fearsome. Indeed they are one of the few animals that regularly regard humans as prey. But thank God they did survive, giving us an insight into an animal way of life many millions of years old, and still successful in a world dominated by rampaging human animals. It is interesting to note that lions and tigers, for example, are less awesome because they generally steer well clear of mankind. Crocodiles on the other hand have no fear of humans, and when they see a meal they take it, whether it has four legs or two. Its great size and cold blood has always inspired horror in humans.'

We arrived at the crocodile farm, which turned out to be the one that was used in the James Bond movie *Live and Let Die.*

There is a famous sequence in the film where Bond is left stranded on a tiny island, with hordes of hungry crocodiles slowly moving towards him on all sides. The reptiles inadvertently form a line like stepping stones, thus enabling the hero to step hurriedly across from croc to croc and escape. The stunt was carried out by a Jamaican gentleman, who worked on the farm. Two people had arrived from Publicity and they introduced us to him. He proved to be a cheerful, courteous man in his early 40s. Apparently, when he first did the stunt it all went horribly wrong and the crocodiles savaged him. He was lucky to escape with his life and spent many weeks in hospital. When he had recovered he insisted that he should be allowed to attempt the stunt again. He was adamant about it and the film company reluctantly agreed. Much to their relief he pulled it off.

The Jamaican stuntman enthusiastically showed us his scars. They were terrible! Absolutely horrific! God knows how he survived. The scars were long and jagged, you could actually see the teeth marks. Pink and white. They stood out vividly against his dark skin. Both Alf and I gave an involuntary gasp of revulsion, which delighted our Jamaican hero no end! There was not a single area of his body that was free of scars. Three hundred stitches had been needed to sew him up again. Of course, the whole thing had made him a celebrity!

He introduced us to about half a dozen other wardens in the park and they escorted us to a compound of mangroves and palm trees, and several large ponds that were occupied by scores of big American crocodiles (*Crocodylus acutus*). The photographer whose brief it was to do the 'shoot' showed no sign of nerves, accompanied us into the compound and, after flashing us an encouraging smile, set up his tripod and fished from his camera case various lenses for his vast array of cameras. I was very impressed. We stopped about 7 yards (6.5 m) from the somnolent creatures and made ourselves comfortable but very quiet.

To protect us from the reptiles, the wardens were armed with great thick sticks. Nevertheless, I still felt uneasy. At the best of times I am not the fastest man on Earth, and this was not the best of times! I was dressed as Long John Silver – with one leg pinned across my buttocks in a sling! Still, everything seemed peaceful and calm enough, and it was a lovely afternoon.

From outside the 5-foot (1.5 m) metal fence which overlooked us and the pond a friendly, silver-haired gentleman in his mid-60s introduced himself. His name was Kramer, and he was a zoologist from Boston in the USA. He told us that the American crocodile is the only species which is widespread in the Americas. Its range is from Southern Florida (mainly in the Everglades and the Florida Keys) to Venezuela, and the West Coast of Mexico to Ecuador and Northern Peru. It is still found on Cuba, Jamaica, and the Cayman Islands, but not in the Bahamas. Across all this range it is now scarce, because of hunting and habitat destruction. Mr Kramer slightly concerned us, for he seemed to punctuate every sentence with a small, grating cough.

'Are you all right, sir?' I enquired. 'Have you got a cold?'

'No, no,' he replied, politely raising his white 'Tilly' hat with old world charm. 'It's very kind of you to enquire. I guess I ought to explain. I've just spent three months exploring the Orinoco Basin in Venezuela, right through to the Meta river, where I have been studying the Orinoco Crocodile (*Crocodylus intermedius*). First time I saw one my heart skipped a beat, they are a hellava sight! Olive green above and much paler below, it's a freshwater species, preferring slow-flowing rivers or lakes. Like most other crocodiles, it is becoming rare because of hunting. Its skin is more valuable than that of other species which live in the same region. Anyway, I spent about ten hours one evening trying to make my way through a series of cold waterfalls in very rough terrain. I got chilled to my bones and I still haven't recovered. The cough is a goddammed nuisance! It was worth it though. You wanna see my scar? I noticed you were looking at the young man's. Well here is mine!'

With that, he pulled back his sleeve to reveal two large dark marks on his forearm.

'They are the marks of the Labarria (fer de lance), its fangs are over an inch (2.5 cm) long.'

'But a bite from that snake is almost invariably fatal!' I replied, astonished.

'You said it, Mr Blessed, you said it, and heaven knows why I am still alive. I just suppose I'm the luckiest guy in the world. We had two doctors on the expedition and they gave me the serum, or I wouldn't be alive today. I was sick for days. It sure makes you appreciate being alive. Unfortunately, one of the guys on the expedition blew the head off the snake just below the neck. When they examined it its fangs had venom like golden syrup dripping out of the ends. I love snakes, I'm sorry that he killed it.'

'He's as mad as you are,' said Alf.

'Exactly,' I replied, 'a man after my own heart.'

Whereupon, Kramer joined us in 'the lion's den'.

For two hours our colourful guest described every species of crocodile ('crocodilians', he called them) that ever existed. I was fascinated to learn that the largest crocodilian ever known was called deinosuchus (the 'Terror Crocodile'). It lived in the late Cretaceous period in North America and its remains have been found in locations as widely separated as Montana, Texas, Delaware and Georgia, in fossil beds which were laid down some 70 million years ago. Its lower jaw was 7 feet (2 m) long and its length must have been in the region of 50 feet (15 m). Its weight has been estimated at over 6 tons (6.1 tonnes).

'What a monster,' I exclaimed.

'Yes, indeed, Mr Blessed,' Kramer replied, his sapphire blue eyes dancing with delight in the fading sunlight. Kramer was pleased about the progress that had been made in controlling the trade in skins and encouraging captive breeding and other methods of limiting the rate at which reptiles are taken from the wild. Kramer was also pleased that many countries were restoring the wild habitat of crocodiles. He maintained that they are an essential part of the ecosystem of those habitats. But there still remains a great deal to be done. More nature reserves and national parks are needed.

As we moved out of the compound, I asked Kramer why crocodiles are frequently seen lying on the river banks or in streams with their mouths wide open.

He replied, 'Crocodiles do this to lower their temperature, by allowing moisture to evaporate from the lining of their mouth, or in some cases raising it, by exposing this highly vascular lining to the sun. What is puzzling is that it is also seen in the cool of the early morning. Many zoologists think it is either a threat in response to some enemy, or possibly as a way of drying out the lining of the mouth to reduce the chance of infestation by algae of fungi. The fact is, we don't really know. We still have a lot to learn about them.

'For instance, did you know that diamonds have been found in the stomachs of dead crocodiles in Venezuela? The reason for their presence is to aid digestion. They're fascinating creatures. I've been in love with crocodiles since I was a child and I have always wanted to be a zoologist. I suppose my favourite is the Cuban crocodile (*Crocodylus rhombifer*) with its short toes and only vestigially webbed feet. It is the most land-based of the living crocodiles. It frequently moves in a 'high-walk' and can be seen sitting on its haunches with its forelimbs straight, like a dog. Its hide is too heavily armoured to be of any use to the skin trade so it is left in peace. It has a pair of bony crests at the back of its skull which makes it look as though it has horns. It's not that big, about 11 feet (3.4 m) fully grown. But its black, armoured body is covered in yellow spots. Gorgeous! A real dinosaur!'

As we reached his battered old vehicle, he turned and we shook hands.

'It's been a pleasure, Mr Blessed. Hope we meet again soon. Here's a tooth from an old Orinoco crocodile. It will bring you luck when you go to the Lost World. I can see at a glance that you've allowed the child in you to father the man. Stay that way. Be seein' yer.'

I waved a long goodbye, and was sad to see him go.

As I gazed out over the crimson Caribbean Sea, I rejoiced in the thought of just how many varieties of crocodile there are on this planet of ours. They range from the Nile in Egypt, right through mighty Africa to Madagascar. Those 'cold-eyed sweetie-pies', reside in India, Pakistan, Sri Lanka, Bangladesh, the Malay Peninsula, Indonesia, the Philippines, New Guinea, Australia, the Solomon Islands, Figi, Burma, China, Thailand, Kampuchea, Vietnam, Borneo, Sumatra, Nepal, Florida, Mexico, South America and thousands of islands in the blue, green, grey seas of our beautiful Earth.

What hinders crocodile conservation, I thought, is that they are not like koala bears. They are not sweet and cuddly. In a lot of countries they are hated and classified as vermin. What's to be done? I thought. Well, we must be caring and vigilant, and protect this unique relic. After all, they have survived from the age of the dinosaur. They have survived the most appalling catastrophes the Earth has seen. Ice ages, earthquakes, shifting continents, meteors. Yes, they've come through it all unscathed. In fact I concluded on that delightful warm beach, that one cannot separate oneself in any shape or form from the myriad of creatures on this Earth. Kramer had said that the crocodile heart too, is closer to that of a mammal than to those of other reptiles, giving them a more efficient circulatory system. And the famous philosopher, Arthur Koestler, spoke at great length in one of his books about the ancient reptilian part of our brain. Christ! I thought, I'm about to convince myself that I'm a dinosaur! Nevertheless, I mused, surely these admirable, prehistoric reptiles have earned the right to live. For God's sake, let the survivor survive.

'It's farcical,' I said out loud, 'to think that a tiny bipedal mammal, that boasts of having evolved a God-connected conscience, can be so cruel to one of nature's great successes.'

I stopped thinking. And allowed the last rays of sunset to kiss and sweeten my mind. The Jamaican experience was over.

7

THE STONE SENTINEL

On 10 January 1993, I experienced a savage attack from a huge 33-foot (10 m) green salt-water crocodile. What made the experience particular galling was the fact that it was witnessed by over 2,000 people who couldn't be bothered to lift a finger to help me; in fact they appeared to be encouraging the damn beast to devour me. It was horrible! The pain and embarrassment was excruciating. The crocodile had a firm grip on my right arm and was slowly dragging me along the ground towards its lair. I shouted in pain and begged for help, but my pleas fell on deaf ears. I cursed the lot of them and stuck the fingers of my left hand into the reptile's eyes. All to no avail.

A great deal has been written about gastroliths, which are stones and other hard objects found in the stomachs of crocodiles to aid their digestion. Gastroliths recently recovered from crocodiles' stomachs have included footballs, Thermos flasks, radios, and CDs but never, as far as I can ascertain, has anyone ever recovered a ticking clock!

In spite of the pain I was suffering, I was amazed to hear a tick-tock emanating from deep inside the crocodile. I was almost tempted to ask it the time! My incredulity increased, for as I stared deep into the beast's mouth, I came face to face with a charming young lady called Joanne!

'Hello,' I said. 'What's a pretty gastrolith like you doing in a crocodile's mouth?'

Of course, my dear reader, you must have guessed that I was playing Captain Hook in J. M. Barrie's *Peter Pan*. That particular production was at the De Montfort Hall Theatre in Leicester. Kristian Schmid (Todd from *Neighbours*) played Peter Pan, and my wife, Hildegard Neil, played Mrs Darling. The show had been a tremendous success, breaking box-office records, and this was the final performance.

I was sad, but at the same time very excited. After years of expectation, frustration, hope and despair, I was, at last going to South America. Yes indeed! South America! That astonishing, miraculous continent, that so attracted the likes of Pizarro, Baron Alexander Von Humboldt, Eric Shipton, and the young naturalist Charles Darwin. Unfortunately, I was not going to the Lost World, that mysterious part of Venezuela still eluded me. Nevertheless, I felt I was heading in the right direction. After all, Venezuela is South America.

The Andes mountain chain is the longest continuous range in the world extending 4,500 miles (7,200 km) along the western edge of South America. From Colombia to Cape Horn more than forty active volcanoes, some soaring to over 20,000 feet (6,096 m) testify to the deep subterranean forces still shaping the Andes. These active regions are linked by other extinct cones to form the longest and highest chain on the active volcano belt called 'the Girdle of Fire', which encircles the Pacific Ocean. Standing supreme in this wild landscape of gigantic mountains is mighty Aconcagua at 22,830 feet (6,958 m). Aconcagua is the highest mountain in South America, indeed in the western hemisphere, and the highest mountain outside Asia.

I had been invited to join an expedition to climb it organized by a company called Himalayan Kingdoms and led by a terrific climber called Steve Bell, who was 31 years of age. It is said that 'a leader must be a step above the angels' and Steve shares this distinction with the likes of Chris Bonington, David Breashers, the American climber, and Lord Hunt. I had trained very hard for this expedition and desperately wanted to reach the summit. In a way I was using it as a dress rehearsal for climbing Mount Everest, though in no way was I underestimating the difficulties of climbing Aconcagua. It was going to be a tough, arduous climb.

I was now 57 years old, and three years earlier I had made a film with the BBC called *Galahad of Everest*, in which I had worn similar clothes to those of the first Everestiers of the early 1920s. On that occasion I reached a height of 25,500 feet (7,772 m) on the North Ridge of Everest. The film was a tribute to George Leigh Mallory and Andrew Irvine who disappeared on the mountain in 1924. On that occasion we had no intention of climbing Everest, our objective was simply to make a film about the two heroes. Now, in 1993, I was to return to the Himalayas in March to try to climb the mountain from the southern side.

Aconcagua would be a stiff test and would show me whether I was fit enough for Everest. I felt confident about it but, of course, the experts and the boring Doubting Thomases said it was foolish of me at my age to attempt such an undertaking. They maintained that I was too old. But as my Yorkshire father would frequently say, 'I took no gorm on 'em!'

To any older reader, all I can say is, don't be put off by people telling you that you are too old. It's not how old you are but how you are old. Nothing's impossible.

When Peter Habeler first climbed Everest without oxygen with Reinhold Messner, he said, 'What the doubting physiologists fail to recognize is the mysterious "X factor" that everyone possesses.'

Mind you, as David Breashears says, 'Ya gotta want it.' And you certainly have to be very, very fit before you attempt to climb a mountain like Aconcagua.

Running is absolutely essential, you have to run and run like the Red Dogs in Kipling's *The Jungle Book*. Cycling and swimming too are ideal exercise for getting into top condition. The main emphasis is on cardiovascular improvement. If you remember, Tenzing Norgay, who first climbed Everest, got fit by filling his rucksack with small rocks and climbing steep hills around his home. Long-distance walks with a rucksack weighing 44 pounds (20 kg) or more are enormously beneficial. The idea that you can get fit on the approach march to the mountain is sheer nonsense. A good level of fitness before the expedition certainly gives you the best chance of achieving the summit. Also, it is vital not to 'peak-out' in fitness before the expedition but to slowly increase your overall state of fitness right up to departure.

Nevertheless, the best laid plans of mice and men can come unstuck. To be honest, in spite of my best intentions, I have never been fully prepared for any expedition that I have embarked on, there is always so much to do and so little time to do it in. My study at home, on this occasion, looked as though it had been ransacked by a dozen yetis: tents, sleeping bags, rucksacks, plastic boots, gloves, jackets, hats, ski-poles, ice-axes and scores of other items littered the floor and furniture. I would fill a rucksack one minute, and empty it the next.

'Where's my torch? Where's the medical kit? Christ, my rucksack is going to weigh a bloody ton!' All this was addressed to my PA, who bore it all with a patient smile and calmed me down with cups of tea.

Unfortunately, doing the pantomime in Leicester had taken the edge off my training. I actually thought that I could continue running 10 miles (16 km) a day and doing power weights in the gym, whilst I was performing as Captain Hook, twice daily. It just wasn't possible. The pantomime took up all my time. If I wasn't performing, then I was doing interviews and publicity for the show.

To top it all, my PA, Stephen, then reminded me that I had not checked with my doctor whether my vaccinations were up-to-date. Steve Bell, the expedition leader, said on the phone, 'Brian, you may also wish to consider having jabs for hepatitis B, tuberculosis, meningitis and rabies.'

'Rabies, Steve,' I replied, 'You must be bloody joking.'

'No, Brian, there are lots of wild dogs in the vicinity of Aconcagua.'

Well, I thought, if the mountain doesn't kill me, the jabs will!

In the weeks before departure I had started to drink large quantities of water to get my body used to forcing it down on the mountain. Increased water intake facilitates adaptation to altitude and helps your kidneys excrete excess salts, which bind extra water in the tissues. So, what with jabs, water intake, checking my gear and the concern about my fitness levels, I ended up in a right state. Beneath it all I was simply scared. This always happens when I am about to go on an expedition. The worst time is two or three days before departure when all kinds of doubts enter my mind.

The duration of the expedition was twenty-five days and we were due to leave London on 8 January, arriving back on 1 February. There was a slight problem. I would not be able to join until 12 January because of my commitment to *Peter Pan*. This meant that I would have less time to acclimatize than the other members of the expedition. Still, I comforted myself with the fact that I had always performed well at altitude. But it also meant that I would be travelling on my own, which was a pity because I always enjoyed flying with the other members of an expedition and getting to know them.

When I had finished the last performance of the pantomime, my wife and I hastily made our way home down the M1 and arrived back in Surrey in the early hours of the morning. There to greet us was our army of barking dogs. I was going to miss them! I was homesick already.

By the way, this is a genuine problem on a mountain – homesickness. It can stop a mountaineer from reaching the summit.

The following morning I was in a right tizz! I hadn't finished packing. Stephen calmed me down with more tea and checked everything for me while I went for a 'quick' 5-mile (8 km) run around nearby Lightwater Country Park. On my return I hugged every dog and cat, blew kisses to the ponies, ducks, hens and fish, and last but not least I held my pretty 16-year-old daughter Rosalind in a big bear hug. Then, quick as a flash, Stephen and Hildegard bundled me into our ageing Space Wagon and whisked me off around the M25 to Heathrow.

Before you could say 'Bob's yer Uncle' I was on board Aerolineas Argentinas Flight 171 bound for Buenos Aires. In my mind's eye I saw Hildegard's beautiful face and grey-green eyes and Stephen's handsome face and bright blue eyes smiling and waving in friendly reassurance.

Hours later, when the sun had fallen out of the sky and the dark cloak of night had finally spread its mantle, I felt bewitched by the thought of the mysterious continent below. The animals of the night would be awake now. The dark virgin rain forests would be pulsating with the high-pitched sounds of trillions of rejoicing neon insects, and yellow, red and bright blue frogs would be croaking boastfully across the Orinoco river. In the fertile grasslands of Llanos, large anacondas would be hissing and honking at the energetic, skilled horsemen, the llaneros. Heavy rain would be feeding the Amazon tributaries from north of the Equator to the Tropic of Capricorn. On the high-dry desert of the Altiplano, Aymara Indians, who farm the harsh shores of the silvery Lake Titicaca, would be paying homage by their campfires to their bearded god Viracocha, who rose from the waters' great depth to establish their culture. In deepest Ecuador, the violent volcano Sangay, known as the 'Flaming Terror', would be blasting out bombs, whose shrapnel was lava, ash and steam. In El Dorado, goldminers would be weighing their precious yellow dust and counting the cost of their week's labour, as malaria and dengue fever attacked their red blood corpuscles. Deep in the Amazonas, protective soldier ants would be performing their nightly ritual and rolling thousands of precious diamonds around the white bones of the lost explorer Colonel P. H. Fawcett. Shamans, deep in the Matto Grosso, would be conversing with the ghosts of Inca kings, whilst on the summit of Roraima, the Goddess Kuin would be blessing her nightly visitors with *Kachiri* liquor and soothing their senses with the music of the *tepui*'s winds. On the ice-cap of Patagonia, fierce winds would be chilling the souls of climbers retreating from awesome Cerro Fitzroy. And in the heart of the high Andes, the guardian of three elements, mighty Aconcagua, was awaiting the Himalayan Kingdoms Expedition from Britain.

At this point in the journey I switched off all the lights in the various rooms of my brain and slept like a baby. Several hours later I woke up, had breakfast, fastened my seat belt and touched down in Buenos Aires where I was met by a car from the organizers of the expedition.

Buenos Aires is the largest city on the South American continent. Through the window of the car it looked cheerful and spacious. Cruising along the wide and beautiful Avenue General Peron, we passed several pretty wooded parks and eventually arrived at our destination, the Hotel Principado. Here I was able to relax for a few hours before being collected and then taken on to the domestic airport, Aeroparque.

The flight was due to leave at 4.10 in the afternoon and was destined to arrive fifty minutes later in Mendoza. The flight was absolutely delightful. We flew over the Pampas, which stretched away for hundreds of miles in every direction, a gigantic patchwork of cultivated fields, crops and vast prairies, where hundreds of cows were peacefully grazing.

Gradually and almost imperceptibly the cultivated land changed to rocky desert with sand dunes and isolated clumps of stunted shrubs. The plane was now very close to the Andes, but the range was hidden behind a thick curtain of storm cloud, and so Aconcagua remained invisible.

The plane made a 'hands, knees and bumpsy-daisy' landing on to the concrete runway of Mendoza. The little town has the reputation of being one of the prettiest in Argentina. A charming oasis at the foot of barren mountains.

It had been arranged that I should stay the night in Mendoza and set off with a guide the following morning to catch up with the rest of the expedition. They were several days ahead of me.

I had a mouth-watering dinner. Meat in Argentina is sensational! It must be all that pampas grass that the cattle eat. Then I went for a stroll around Mendoza. This quaint provincial town is famous for its wine and it reminded me of some of the villages I had seen in southern Spain. Children played happily in the streets and in the central piazza, whilst their parents dined *al fresco* and laughed and conversed about the events of the day. I bought myself a large chocolate ice-cream cornet and contentedly mooched around the shops, humming like a 4-year-old.

Back at the hotel I sat on the veranda and drank a delicious milky coffee. It was a clear night and in the distance I could see the dark outline of the mighty Andes.

This is probably as good a time as any to give you a brief history of Aconcagua. As I said before, it is the highest point in the western hemisphere, and the highest mountain outside Asia. It lies just inside the border with Chile, to the east of the actual Andes, in the small frontal range. It is 22,830 feet

(6958 m) high, and it has two summits joined by a ridge – the Cresta Del Guanaco – which is approximately 0.6 miles (1 km) long. Other ridges radiate from each summit and the whole massif is isolated from other peaks. Shaped like a gigantic wedge, it has a very steep and massive face to its south and a gentle slope to the north.

The huge Polish Glacier flows to the east and a series of arêtes and couloirs flank it on the west. Rising from a massive base, like most of the Andes giants, it dominates its highest rivals by 4,920 feet (1,500 m). It is visible from the Pacific Ocean 106 miles (170 km) away, and the Chilean towns of Santiago and Valparaiso are virtually in its shadow.

The power of the Incas extended right down the continent of South America. From the time of the legendary Cuzco, they ascended the valley of Uspallata, reached the base of Aconcagua which they christened 'Acconcahua' or 'Ackon-Cahuac', made up of the words 'Ackon' (of stone) and 'Cavac' (he who watches). It is this name – the Stone Sentinel – which is still borne today by this guardian of three elements: ocean, sky and pampas.

What is not generally known is that in 1817 general Don Jose De San Martin was the first to experience the terrors of the Stone Sentinel. South America was in the process of shaking off the yoke of the Spanish conquerors and Argentine territory was already liberated. Martin decided to cross the Andean chain at its highest point in the region of Mount Mercedario, Aconcagua and Tunpungato.

In all, 5,300 men, 10,600 mules and 1,600 horses travelled the passes at a height of 13,120 feet (3,999 m). Dragging their guns and equipment over endless slopes of frozen scree and ice, whipped and scoured by fierce winds of over 100 miles per hour (160 kph), their throats parched, and frostbitten by cold and lack of humidity resulting from the altitude, the soldiers of San Martin successfully overcame all obstacles. But the bodies of 6,300 mules and 1,100 horses lined the route from Uspallata to Chile, bearing silent testimony to the suffering endured by this amazing army.

The first known attempt on Aconcagua was by a German mountaineer, Paul Gussfeldt, in 1883. A man with a will of iron, Gussfeldt undertook this terrible task of attempting to climb its tremendous interminable slopes with inadequate equipment and a few Chilean porters with no climbing experience at all.

Early in February 1883, the German climber left Santiago. It was a long and arduous route to Aconcagua, but nothing daunted him, he launched two bold assaults on the summit. The first one was the most successful and took him to a height of 21,480 feet (6,547 m), just 1,400 feet (43 m) from the summit! But because of bad weather and exhaustion his porters deserted him and he was forced to beat a desperate retreat for his life.

On his second attempt he did not get as high and had to concede defeat once again.

Mountaineers often say that the ascent of Aconcagua is more a survival test than anything else. Bad footing on loose shale, bitter winds, frostbite and thin air all combine to exhaust its would-be conquerors.

In 1896, a party led by the noted alpinist Edward Fitzgerald approached the mountain. This expedition included a team of Swiss and Italian guides led by the already famous Mathias Zubriggen. Fitzgerald wanted a very strong party, and he was furnished with ample, carefully chosen equipment. This was just as well, for Aconcagua soon revealed itself as one of the toughest and most ruthless adversaries climbers of that era had ever had the temerity to attack.

They spent months on its slopes, so overcome by mountain sickness, cold and fierce winds they could barely find the strength to climb. In one of their main assaults everybody, except Fitzgerald and Zubriggen, turned back exhausted at 16,000 feet (4,877 m). Step by step the two heroes toiled up the apparently endless shifting scree and made camp at about 17,000 feet (5,182 m). The next day, after 2 hours, they reached 19,025 feet (5,799 m). A storm was brewing and Fitzgerald had reached exhaustion point. The retreat was on. Battered by furious squalls, the two only just escaped with their lives.

Weeks later the entire party made another attempt from base camp. Once more the pitiless wind scourged them, growing colder and more furious with every step up the steep slopes. The powerful Zubriggen collapsed with badly frozen feet. Vigorous rubbing partially restored circulation, but once again they were forced with more difficulty than ever to beat a retreat. Weeks of abject suffering and failure followed.

In a last valiant assault the expedition reached 21,975 feet (6,698m), less than 1,000 feet (300 m) from the summit. After a short rest Fitzgerald endeavoured to struggle to his feet but he was exhausted. This man with the courage of a lion had found his master. He ordered Zubriggen to go on alone, and a wreck of his former self, he turned back with the guides Pollinger and Lanti.

Amazingly, for the third time, Zubriggen found himself alone on the mountain. Jaded with fatigue, he tenaciously continued the climb foot by foot, and after surmounting a short rocky wall, he was there; the miracle was performed! There was nothing above him; the Southern Hemisphere and the two Americas were at his feet. A cairn and an ice-axe erected on the summit remained as mute witness of the first victory of man over the Stone Sentinel of the Incas.

That is the mountain I was about to attempt to climb.

Our first view of the Lost World.

The track to Roraima.

Kukenan River, a tough obstacle to cross on the way to Roraima.
In the background is the mighty Kukenan.

Sporadic white clouds hang motionless against the cliffs of Roraima.

'We were within seven miles from an enormous line of ruddy red cliffs which encircled, beyond all doubt, the plateau of which Professor Challenger spoke.' *The Lost World*

Beginning the ascent of Roraima through tropical rainforest.

Halfway up Roraima's green mansions.

'Roraima looked haunting and blood-red in the fading light.' *The Lost World*

Medical attention for Maz's foot, near the top of the rainforest.

At last we are through the forest and I can the base of Roraima's cliffs.

On the roof of Roraima.

Pause for a photograph before heading for our high camp.

Exterior view of the Grand Hotel.

Arrival at the Grand Hotel.

Inside the Grand Hotel after my
first sleepless night on Roraima.

The extraordinary rock formations on Roraima's summit,
which create such a haunting landscape.

The vegetation of Roraima.

Spider on the top of Roraima.

Small lake on the rocky landscape of Roraima.

8

BIG YETI

The following morning, after a good night's sleep I was greeted by a tall, raw-boned young man in his early 20s called Francisco.

'I am your guide, Meester Brian,' he said, and flashed a huge Pepsodent smile. He reminded me of the famous old-time film star Caesar Romero and from the off we got on famously. I had my rucksack with me containing all my gear. The rest of my belongings, I placed in my 'Himalayan Kingdoms' bag which the hotel had kindly agreed to take care of.

'Your rucksack is very heavy, Meester Brian,' said Francisco. 'Mine is light, I take some of your tings out and place in mine to help you.'

'Very kind, thank you,' I replied.

'Now we must go. Many miles to travel. The drive to Puente Del Inca is maybe 150 kilometres, how you say – ah – like 100 miles. Not too far, bumpy perhaps, good driver we have. We have plenty of water, and I have coffee too in flask. Good eh?'

'Yes, Francisco,' I said, laughing. 'Lets rock 'n' roll and catch up and even pass the expedition in front of us.'

After a brief introduction to the driver, we jumped into the back of what appeared to be a beaten up, roofless, military command car. I was dressed in light trekking clothes and a floppy green hat held tight about my head by string. I wore my high-altitude glasses as a precaution against the dazzling sunlight, and we set off. It was 7.00 a.m.

We left Mendoza and its suburbs behind and got on to a wide concrete road that went straight as an arrow for some 20 miles (32 km). It was a pleasure to drive along it. I contemplated the spectacle before me.

The great arid plain was devoid of any sign of vegetation, apart from the inevitable cacti. Francisco pointed out over to the left an old Indian trail leading from Mendoza to Uspallata. A little further on, the road turned to the west and entered the mountains. It was no longer concrete and the driver took us somewhat too enthusiastically around hazardous hairpin bends! The scenery changed abruptly and a Cyclopean landscape presented itself. Enormous outcrops and huge bastions of disintegrated rock appeared on all sides and I tied my silk scarf over my nose and mouth to protect me from the clouds of dust thrown up by our vehicle.

The deeply cut gorges of these intimidating mountains were now covered in cacti that looked like aliens from space. There were thousands of them, all strangely static and over 6 feet (1.8 m) in height, giant candelabra with their large white 'candles' reflecting the sun's light and bristling with spikes 5 or 6 inches (12–15 cm) long. Francisco said that it was not advisable to touch these spikes, as they were so hard that the Indians, after boring a hole through them, used them as needles.

Leaving this bizarre landscape behind, we arrived in a tiny valley through which splashed a little stream surrounded by numerous trees and surprisingly well-kept lawns. We had come across a mini 'Shangri-La'. This enchanting oasis of delight formed a magical background to the Spa Hotel of Villavicencio.

We were approaching 8,200 feet (2,499 m) and the cacti were receding. At 9,500 feet (2,896 m) we reached a col, where the road crossed the foothills of the Andes. As we rounded a bend I was shattered by the enormous number of *cordilleras* – thousands of peaks, separated by deep valleys. There were no trees, no forests, I couldn't even see a blade of grass. An astonishing chaos of rocks, plateaus, aretes, scree, precipices and distant snow-tipped mountains. Reds of every shade, greens, blues, yellows, browns, black and white, merged into one another on the mountains and valleys of this mind-blowing wilderness. It was like a Martian landscape, and there above the universe of rocks soared the summit of Aconcagua, proudly asserting its undoubted supremacy.

I asked them to stop the car for a few moments, to allow me to take in the overwhelming splendour of it all. The Stone Sentinel banished all thought. Wide-eyed and tearful I touched the driver's shoulder and we sped on. Francisco was noticeably pleased at my reaction to the mountain. He pointed out a pampas ostrich in the distance and said that there were lots of armadillos and wild horses in the region.

We now descended a pass at breakneck speed which scared the pants off me. The driver took all the curves at great speed. Francisco didn't bat an eyelid and smiled reassuringly. It was all in a day's work!

At last, and to my great relief, the steep slope eased off and after a short while we reached the village of Uspallata. Once more I was pleasantly surprised, for the presence of water had made this too a tiny 'Shangri-La'. We stopped and drank coffee under some weeping willows that lined the roadside, while an army of officials examined my papers. After a cursory glance, they gave me the official nod, and we were on our way again.

We had covered about 60 miles (96 km) since leaving Mendoza and had a further 50 miles (80 km) or so to go before we would reach Puente del Inca. After leaving the village, the valley of the Mendoza river opened out before us. Down this valley flowed all the water from the slopes of Aconcagua. Gigantic slopes of multicoloured scree rose up on both sides of the valley. The peaks up above were over 16,000 feet (5,568 m). We were on the threshold of the *cordilleras*. The road now began the long climb to Puenta del Inca. Over to the left could be seen the snow cone of Tupangata, the second highest summit of the Andes. We continued up the central valley and arrived at a small cemetery, where rest the many victims of Aconcagua. It was a sobering moment, and made me realize once again what a serious undertaking Aconcagua was. For here lay the remains of Argentine, British, Yugoslav and American citizens and many others. Presently we saw a sign indicating the entrance to Puenta del Inca and after a short while our driver stopped at the military outpost. This time I was put through the hoop. The officers questioned me about everything. One of them appeared contemptuous of my age.

'Feeefty-seven?'

I glared at him like a thunderclap. For a moment he must have thought I was going to assault Francisco because I slid my hand between his legs and grabbed his buttocks. At the same time, with my other hand, I gripped his left shoulder and lifted him above my head.

'Fifty-seven,' I roared. 'Fifty-seven years is Sweet Fanny Adams.'

This broke the ice and the soldiers applauded my snatch and lift with great enthusiasm, although they had no idea who 'Sweet Fanny Adams' was. We left them in the best of spirits and I promised to bring them back some rock from the summit of Aconcagua. Five minutes later we arrived at our destination.

Puenta del Inca is the last inhabited place on the road to Aconcagua and stands at an altitude of 8,850 feet (2,697 m). It gets its name from a natural bridge of rock, which spans the muddy waters of the river Las Cuevas. This amazing rock is pinkish in colour and looks as though it has been placed there by some giant from antiquity. The hot springs nearby have deposited a limestone covering of brilliant yellow. These springs, which petrify anything in the course of three weeks, are renowned throughout Argentina for their therapeutic properties. They cure rheumatism and nervous ailments. Inca legend has it that one of them, the 'Spring of Love', has a salutary effect upon your sex life.

I found it a very beautiful and fascinating place, which I fancied was haunted by Inca spirits. Anyway, it was now time to head off on foot into the wilderness.

I thanked the driver and gave him a decent tip and, after tightening my boots and adjusting the straps of my rucksack, we set off towards the Horcones Valley. The expedition, which was roughly two days ahead of us, had camped a day earlier at Horcones Lake at the entrance to the valley and it was about a four-hour march from Puenta del Inca. They would now be setting off for their next camp at Confluencia, four hours further on.

As its name suggests, Confluencia is at the junction of the two Horcones valleys: the upper descends from the northern slopes of Aconcagua, and the lower has its source on the south side. Our noble leader, Steve Bell, had left the choice to me. Either Francisco and I could camp at Lake Horcones, or make a very long day of it and go to Confluencia. The latter option would involve eight hours or so of tough walking at a height of between 9,000 and 10,000 feet (2,743–3,048 m). Nevertheless I decided on Confluencia.

I turned to a pensive Francisco and said, 'Bollocks! Let's go for it. You and me, Francisco, we'll show the expedition how to walk. Let's rock 'n' roll!'

'Yes,' shouted my new-found Argentinean friend, 'Yes, Mr Brian, bollocks! We go for it! Let's rock 'n' roll!'

With that we set off like a couple of bats out of hell, though I have to say, I had to slow him down a little. He was very fast! He was only 22 and this journey was something he did many times during the year. He was fully acclimatized and his natural turn of speed was aided by his very long legs.

In the cold morning air the Stone Sentinel looked higher and more distant than ever. It was about 10.00 a.m. After a few hours we reached Lake Horcones and paused for a ten-minute break to eat some boiled eggs, a Granola bar and some sweet coffee. We felt exhilarated by our surroundings. With Aconcagua's reflection swimming in the calm waters of the lake, we pressed on and passed the stream

El Duragno, where the rough path began to steepen until even Francisco gasped for breath, but we didn't pause and ploughed on energetically for Confluencia.

Far to our right we could clearly see Mount Almacen at 16,700 feet (5,090 m). Almacen means 'shop', so named because the horizontal and regular arrangement of its strata resembles shelving. To our left was Tolosa which was even higher, at 17,815 feet (5,450 m). We were now truly in the 'land of the giants'. The valley had started to narrow and the path began to mount a steep scree slope. Two hours later we turned a sharp corner and walked slap bang into the expedition.

I was gobsmacked. They were gobsmacked. It was great. Terrific. So unexpected. 'Big Yeti,' roared John Knowles, throwing his arms around me. I was nick-named Big Yeti on the BBC Everest Expedition in 1990. 'Big Yeti,' John repeated again, breathlessly. 'We didn't expect to see you yet. Bloody marvellous! You've legged it here damn quick. Great to see you, you old bugger! Welcome to the 1993 Aconcagua Expedition!'

John Knowles was co-leader of the expedition. Of course, he would be the first to admit that he is not quite in the same league as Steve Bell. Steve is without doubt one of the leading climbers in the British Isles. Nevertheless, John had built up a fine reputation as a trek leader, who had climbed many mountains throughout the world. But he had never been to the height of Aconcagua and he passionately wanted to get up this one. You could walk from John O'Groats to Land's End and you would never meet a nicer man than John Knowles. At the time he was about 40 years of age, of medium stature, with a smiling face and dancing childlike eyes. He wore spectacles which he constantly took off to clean between bouts of laughter. Amidst all the happy confusion of erecting tents stood Steve Bell. Tall, handsome, blond and blue-eyed with a fair complexion, he embodied everything that one could hope for in a leader. It was astonishing to realize that this young man had twenty years' mountaineering experience behind him. Quick as a flash John introduced me to all the members of the expedition. They were a mixed bunch: a geophysicist, a geologist, a marketing executive, a plant operative, a lawyer and several company directors. Two ladies and ten men. Twelve in all, not including our two very important guides, Daniel Alessio and Mauricio Fernandez, who were up ahead setting up base camp.

I shared a tent with Steve and after swapping stories about llamas, mountains and yetis, we fell asleep. The following morning I was greeted by a member of our team called Lee Nobman. 'How are you big guy?' he said, thumping me in the chest. Lee was 42 years old and was a company director of the Golden State Lumber Company in Vallejo, in the Napa Valley in California in the good old US of A. To write in his own vernacular, 'he was a great guy'. He was of medium height, with a very impressive physique. His short-cropped, thick hair had prematurely greyed. In fact, it was almost white. This, with his ruddy features, short white beard and blazing blue eyes, made him look very distinguished. The white didn't age him a bit. I was also delighted to see that apart from myself, there were two other golden oldies on the expedition. David Goode from Bridgwater in Somerset, who was 60, and a retired company director, and David Martin Jenkins, 51 and also a company director. Incidentally, David is the brother of Christopher Martin Jenkins, the cricket commentator. The two ladies, Ruth Exley and Elizabeth Ponds, were 30. I'll introduce the other members of the expedition as we go along.

We had a leisurely breakfast, and, after striking camp, slowly made out way upwards towards base camp. It would take us about 6 hours, and we would reach an altitude of about 14,000 feet (4,267 m). This would be a considerable increase for me as I had only just arrived from 8,000 feet (2,438 m). The others had been up to 13,120 feet (3,999 m) at Plaza Francia, which was the base camp for expeditions that attempt the south face of Aconcagua. Bearing all this in mind, I decided to take it easy and moved to the rear of our party. Steve joined me, and approved of my decision. It was a lovely still cold morning. The peaks of Dedos and Mexico, all exceeding 16,500 feet (5,029 m), limited our vision to the left. These high red and grey mountains are vast ruins of disintegrating rock towers. 'Love to climb those Steve, and Mount Tolosa further to the left when we return from Aconcagua,' I said. Steve's face lit up. 'Yes, Brian,' he laughed, 'If we've got time, I'd love to. But I must remind you that we have the big one to climb first and it's going to test us all. You can get terrible storms on Aconcagua. The mountain has claimed many lives. But we are a strong team and Daniel and Mauricio are good men.'

For the next hour or so we said nothing, periodically pausing to eat energy bars and drink water. During one of these pauses the words of Himalayan Kingdoms' dossier came to mind: 'The detrimental effects of "cultural pollution" cannot be over-emphasised. The answer is to leave no trace of your passing. Where other cultures and customs are involved, remember that you are a guest in such communities. Respect sensitive areas such as religious sites, the dignity of the simple rural folk that you encounter and local practices where you might unwittingly cause offence. "Take nothing but photographs . . . leave nothing but footprints . . . kill nothing but time".'

'God! How did you remember that?' said Steve.

'I'm an actor, Steve, it's my job.'

But that answer is not strictly accurate. I've always been able to remember past events in my life. This gift that I have been given for recall has always amazed my friends. I'm not claiming I'm special, it's just something that happens. At times it can be quite irritating, both for me and for the people around me. You could say it was a mental pest. Generally, though, it is a blessing and makes me happy. I have for 30 years practised a simple form of meditation that is related to the *Shankacharya* of Northern India. This practice gives me peace. It also activates my memory on many levels. That's all! That is why in this book I am able to remember so many conversations and events.

We were now approaching base camp. We had set off at 9 a.m. and eventually, after ascending some steep scree slopes, we arrived at 3 p.m. There to greet us were Daniel and Mauricio, and Daniel's pretty girlfriend Isabella. They plied us with hot drinks, and in next to no time served a light meal which was delicious. They had erected a splendid mess tent that was both roomy and comfortable. We secured our own tents and made ourselves at home. I had a tent all to myself, so I was a bit spoilt. Nevertheless, I was glad of it, because I'm a bulky lad and I do take up a lot of room in a two-man tents. I also felt tired. I'd come to 14,000 feet (4,267 m) rather quickly, and decided to go to sleep for several hours to allow my body to adjust. And sleep I did, very deeply.

It was about eight o'clock at night when John Knowles woke me. 'Come on, Big Yeti, it's time for dinner.' I stumbled into the mess tent like a drunkard to everyone's amusement. The meal was terrific and we all got on famously. There wasn't a lemon amongst us and I soon became the butt of every joke. It wasn't long before the playing cards came out. They belonged to John Knowles who introduced everybody to a game called Bluff, which I never understood. I'm useless at cards. But the game produced great merriment and I loved watching them play. I was glad to be with the expedition at last and gradually I started to relax. At the end of the evening we went out into the cold night air and retired to our respective tents. I had forgotten to bring my torch to dinner so Ruth and Elizabeth escorted me to my tent.

'Good night Brian, sleep tight,' they cooed, and disappeared into the night.

I failed to tell you that there were at least ten other expeditions at base camp. Poles, Finns, Germans, Spaniards, Frenchmen, you name the nationality, they were there. Base camps always look the same. This one was probably noisier than most. Certainly, the Finns were noisy sods.

Before zipping myself into my sleeping bag I stuck my head out of the tent to have one last look at my surroundings. It was a still, cloudless night. There, huge and black against the night sky, was the Stone Sentinel. The sight made me gasp and I remembered Steve's words, 'We have the big one to climb first. And it's going to test us all. You can get terrible storms on Aconcagua. The mountain has claimed many lives.' I took one more look and zipped up the tent and buried myself in my sleeping bag.

For a while my mind was so full of mountains that I could not sleep. I tossed and turned in my sleeping bag. Judging by the sound of creaking mattresses I gathered that I was not the only one who was having trouble sleeping. Gradually though, I slipped off and slept well. The following morning at breakfast everybody seemed to be lethargic. Myself included. I noticed Ruth had slightly swollen eyes. During coffee Steve spoke to us. 'As you know, by its very nature this trip may be subject to disruptions beyond our control. This could force some changes to the itinerary. Weather is the greatest factor, and on individuals acclimatization has a major effect. Our schedule allows time for acclimatization, but it is possible that some will have a slower than normal rate of adaptation and may not reach the summit. This mountain is big and high, and has a weather system all of its own. It is notorious for its savage storms. They appear without warning. A great deal of stress is placed on the body when climbing above 6,000 metres [19,680 ft]. In order to minimize the effects of altitude, an adequate acclimatization is paramount. The tried and tested formula for this is to climb high and sleep low. We try to gain no more than 600 metres per day [1,992 ft], thereby increasing altitude exposure during the day, but camping at a lower altitude. Also, we will make two trips between camps with moderate loads, rather than one trip with a heavy one. The symptoms of acute mountain sickness are unpleasant and potentially serious, and can only be relieved by immediate descent.

'Shortness of breath will be evident in everyone. Nausea, lack of appetite, insomnia and headaches are common symptoms and not usually serious, but if they persist, descent is vital. More serious effects and side-effects of the rarefied atmosphere are pulmonary and cerebral oedema (fluid retention in the lungs and brain), hypothermia, exhaustion and frostbite (due not only to cold, but also to a decrease in the amount of oxygen for generating heat). It is important that each of you is aware of his or her own physical condition during the climb, and also, please keep an eye on the welfare of other team members. The expedition leaders will keep a close watch on everyone, including, of course, themselves!'

'I'm glad to hear it,' I responded, 'you look bloody awful to me! I recommend, Steve, that you get down to sea level as quickly as possible and take up water sports.'

'Thank you, Brian,' replied Steve (looking as fit as a fiddle), 'for that morale-boosting interjection, I'll get my water wings straight away!'

9

THE PUSH TO THE SUMMIT

For the next few days we ascended and descended in perfect harmony and achieved all our objectives. We had carried loads to Canadian Place at 16,500 feet (5,029 m) as I mentioned, and Nido Condores (Condor's Nest) at 17,100 feet (5,334 m). We also reached Berlin Huts at 19,100 feet (5,821 m). Berlin Huts were built in the 1950s by President Juan Peron. Almost four decades later they still provide climbers with welcome shelter and are generally used as a last overnight point before the assault on the summit. I've not mentioned three other members of our expedition. Sorry lads! They were Stephen Wykes, a geophysicist 38 years of age from Northampton, Chris Clayton, 35, a geologist from Teddington, and John Beckett, 30, a lawyer from Edinburgh. I remember that everyone pestered Beckett for advice throughout the expedition. They were all good lads and true. You might say they were the egg-heads of our party. And that, as I used to say in the West End musical *Cats,* 'completes the naming of cats'.

We were now finally ready to make an attempt on the summit. The weather had been good, 'had' being the operative word. At 4 p.m. on the twelfth day of the trip, large black clouds swept over the crests of the distant mountains. A few days earlier Aconcagua had been bathed in golden sunlight, its white crest framed between gigantic walls. Now it looked black and forbidding. The signs were not good. 'Well, boys, it looks ruddy awful,' said David Goode. A trek had arrived at base camp, their supplies carried by mules. That evening the mules seemed restless, and I could hear their chains rattling. They made such a din that it seemed they were trying to escape. I didn't like this, for when animals are restless it means they sense danger. To add doom and gloom to the proceedings, we heard that two climbers had died of cold and exhaustion on the Polish Glacier, close to our route.

Also, some climbers from other expeditions had returned to base camp suffering from cerebral oedema. We were a quiet bunch of yetis that evening in the mess tent. I broke the silence by spelling out the gruesome details in a husky northern accent, ending with the words of an old Yorkshire comedian, 'It's being so cheerful that keeps me going.' Everyone laughed, but their eyes remained fixed and uneasy, as the west wind belted our tent.

The following morning, it had stopped. It was cold, yes, but the barometer was holding steady. We were ready for the off.

There was no doubt at all that apart from Steve, Daniel, Mauricio and the assistant guides, the two stars of the expedition were Ruth and Elizabeth. As Lee Nobman so succinctly put it, 'They were pretty darn good.' How right he was. Both pretty girls, and darn good. They were fast and they were fit. They were soon a long way ahead of us. At my fittest I couldn't compete with these remarkable girls. But I did now feel fully acclimatized, and I was determined to give them a run for their money. It was great fun and it brought a lightness to the proceedings that gave us temporary respite from the tragedies that had occurred on the mountain. We were at about 16,000 feet (4,877 m), with the ladies about 500 feet (150 m) ahead of us when I started to put a spurt on. Steve Bell, who always stayed with the slower party, was sitting on a boulder drinking some coffee when I passed him. He laughed and said, 'I thought you told me you were going to climb like a tortoise.' 'Bugger that,' I said. 'I've changed my mind. I'm going to have a sex change and join the women.' And off I went, motoring along at a fair lick, and in good spirits. The weather was good, and the air tasted wonderful.

After about 20 minutes I caught up with the ladies. We fell silent as we took in our impressive surroundings. We were at Nido Condores at 17,100 feet (5,212 m) and the fresh breeze had increased in strength so I put on my outer Duva jacket.

Temperature drops at a rate of 1°C every 600 feet (182 m) of altitude gained. Our main worry, however, was the wind. Wind causes the body to lose heat far more quickly and it can make a remarkable difference to one's performance.

The rest of the party joined us and during the respite, Steve and Daniel decided that the weather would hold and so we set off for Berlin Huts. The terrain was steeper now and we encountered quite a lot of deep snow. We had been climbing for about five hours and there was still about two hours of climbing left before we would reach Berlin. Aconcagua is a slog!

But, I was still enjoying myself and felt in good form. What a marvellous privilege, I thought, to be climbing such a wonderful mountain.

Steve and Daniel were full of care for members of the team and in moments of despair, they were always on hand with a smile and an encouraging word. We felt secure under their leadership. John Knowles, who had been so kind and attentive lower down the mountain, was now beginning to slow down. The wind had increased and the temperature was plummeting. The strong Scot, Jeffrey Swinney, had kindly offered to stay back with John to give him a helping hand if he needed it.

'You all right, John?' I asked.

He smiled and courageously said, 'I'm all right, Big Yeti, I'll make it.'

We were all relieved when we finally saw the Berlin Huts against the white snowy background. Steve and Daniel pointed to the left to a sheltered spot just a little higher than the huts.

'We'll camp there,' shouted Steve. 'The huts are in an appalling state. There's crap everywhere.'

We had hell getting the tents up. Ugly looking clouds were streaming across the great ridges, and strong gusts of wind pounded us and made it difficult to remain upright. A guy rope broke with a crack like a whip and the tent shook like a demented butterfly in the wind. I had a plastic shovel and worked like a beaver, piling heaps of snow against the tents. By the time I had finished you could hardly see the tents for snow.

Move them if you can, you bastard wind, I thought.

The others were securing ropes and liens with bits of rock and blocks of ice. We were a good team, that was for sure.

'You are sharing a tent with Brian,' Steve shouted to David Martin Jenkins. He looked shocked, he didn't like the idea at all.

'Get in the tent, David,' I roared, 'and unpack our gear. I'm going to help John.'

Steve was busy securing the ladies' tent and gave me a nod of approval. John was having a tough time in the wind and still had a fair distance to cover before he could reach the tents. Jeffrey was alongside him, assisting him all the way. I gradually made my way over to them and took John's rucksack.

'Give me that, you sexy beast,' I shouted. But I couldn't get a smile out of him. He was cold and knackered.

'Come on, John, not far to go, we'll have you in a sleeping bag in next to no time.'

He muttered, 'Thank you, Brian, thank you.'

'That's all right, my son, we'll soon have you there.'

Ten minutes later he was in his tent, out of the wind, and Jeffrey started boiling a brew. I returned to David Martin Jenkins.

I unzipped the tent and presented myself, a snow-covered, red-faced bull.

'David,' I said quietly, 'don't be alarmed about being billeted with me. You will discover that I am actually a very quiet, private man. I love silence. Now and again I will play my cassette recorder. I enjoy classical music. Truth be told I'm a bit of a monk. Don't feel under any obligation to talk to me, all right?'

It was the start of a brief but sweet friendship. Because of my bizarre behaviour in the mess tent, he half expected me to race round our tent, stark naked, growling like King Kong. He was a perfect English gentleman, kind and gentle, and sensitive. David was also a tough individual and deceptively fit. I say deceptively, because he was very thin. He had a high forehead, and his pensive, quizzical face, frequently creased into a smile. I gathered that he was devoted to his church in Haselmere, Surrey.

Much to his delight, over the next three days, it was he, rather than I who started any conversations. Yes, my dear readers, three days!

For as David and I settled into our tent on that first night, the air on the high part of the Stone Sentinel cooled and became dense and heavy and flew downwards with terrifying power, like Thor's hammer, subjecting us to a katabatic (downhill) wind. We saw nature raw in tooth and nail and we realized how impotent we were in the face of these savage manifestations.

The cold was dreadful, and the icy air we breathed seemed devoid of life. The tent was constantly flattened against our faces, so that we had to spend hours holding it up with our hands and ice-axes to be able to breath. Cooking was a nightmare. Going outside to the toilet was a frightful undertaking. It took hours to get back the use of our hands. I had never experienced anything like it.

Each morning, after sunrise, early morning turbulence would create masses of cumulus clouds over the mountain. These quickly built into towering storm clouds that brought violent jet-stream winds of 80–100 miles per hour (128–160 kph) that swept around us into a whirling maelstrom of death. Anyone caught out in such a storm wouldn't last five minutes. It was rough. But our spirits and our tents stood firm.

On the second day, the zip of our tent opened and Steve Bell manoeuvred himself into our presence. Unzipping his Duva jacket, he presented us with a simple meal in plastic bags that had been cooked by Daniel. We couldn't believe it. Visitors in that kind of weather were unheard of, let alone one bearing a cooked meal!

'You all right?' he enquired.

'Sure, Steve,' we replied. 'We still hope to go for the summit!'

'Good lads,' he responded. 'This bloody awful wind has got to stop sometime. Anyway, enjoy your food, compliments of Daniel.'

With that he zipped up his Duva and disappeared into the night.

On the third day there was a lull in the storm and John Knowles informed me that he was going down. I was very sorry to hear this. As I mentioned, he was such a terrific chap and made everyone feel so happy. I tried to persuade him to go on but he wouldn't have it.

'No, Brian,' he said, 'I've had enough. These storms are bloody terrible. I shiver, even in my sleeping bag. I can't get warm. If I try and go on I'll only slow you down. There is still a very long way to go, an ice field and steep scree, and that bloody awful Canaletto before you reach the summit ridge. I just can't face it. God's speed, Big Yeti! I hope the wind drops and you make it.'

It was sad to see him go. But as the saying goes, 'God give me strength to reach the summit, and God give me the event greater strength to turn back!' John certainly had courage.

Steve now called a powwow.

'If the wind stays like this then we'll set off for the summit at 5.00 a.m. tomorrow. I have to inform you that about 1,000 feet (300 m) up, you will have to pass a dead body. A German climber died from a heart attack two days ago, and the body has not yet been taken down the mountain. Try not to let this unfortunate tragedy detract from your objective. These things happen, but it's not going to happen to us. Of course if the weather deteriorates again we will have to turn back. We still have a few days in hand, but you have to face the possibility that this may be as high as we go. Let's see what the morning brings.'

The following morning at 4.00 a.m. the wind had not increased and Steve and Daniel gave the thumbs up for a summit push. We were all tired from lack of sleep, but the news cheered us, and we prepared to leave.

Now look, ladies and gentlemen! If you can't stand swearing, or you are offended by descriptions of our more basic functions, then I recommend you skip the next page or two. All I can say is, I fully sympathize. Several years ago I was staying in Dharamshala in India, the home of the Dalai Lama. I asked an old monk there why he wanted to achieve enlightenment. He answered, 'Because I don't always want to come back to earth as a human being. I can't stand bodily functions. I hate going to the toilet.'

I share his sentiments. So imagine my horror when on the morning of the summit push, I was hit by the most awful diarrhoea. It had been extremely difficult during the storm to maintain a decent level of hygiene in the tent and consequently I was hit by some bug. When the time came to depart I informed Steve of my predicament and said I would catch them up later. He looked concerned, but I slapped him on the back and told him to get moving. The morning was dark and cold with a biting wind. I retreated to a corner by an ice serac, and commenced to undress. Over my underwear I wore what can only be described as a large green Babygro. It had zips in the appropriate places. Oh dear! The trouble we mountaineers have with zips! Unfortunately, the zip covering my crutch area would not work. The metal of the zip had tangled with the material of the baby-grow. I attempted delicate subtle manoeuvres and ended up with a good old-fashioned yank! All to no avail. I was frustrated and furious.

'Bloody hell,' I groaned. 'Bloody hell.'

It meant I had to take the whole lot off. There I was at 19,000 feet (5,791 m) in sub-zero temperatures with a wind chill factor of God knows what, as naked as the day I was born. I was in appalling agony. The diarrhoea was terrible. I was mortified. God knows why because there was nobody watching. I don't know which was worse, the pain from the cold, or the pain in my stomach. I even started vomiting. I'm going to die, I thought. I attempted to revive my spirits by swearing. My body heat was down to zero, and I knew that I would soon be unconscious. But my bowels continued to work. I hated it, and I hated myself.

'This is a bloody sick joke,' I roared to the heavens. 'For God's sake give me a break!'

Gradually it did stop, and I dressed. Then when I was about to set off, I was hit amidships again, and the whole ritual of getting undressed had to be repeated. Eventually I stumbled into my tent and took several doses of Immodium. I usually never take such stuff, but I was desperate. It took effect, but gave me terrible stomach cramps. Maybe I'd taken too much! I couldn't remember. All I knew is I had to stop the trots. Desperately I pulled on my rucksack and headed off in the direction the others had taken. They were too far ahead for me to catch up but I came across Steve after a few moments, who was waiting for me. He was none too happy with my style of walking. One minute I'd hold my head up high, and the next I'd plunge it down between my legs, which were wide apart and rubbery. Though I was frozen and in agony, and resembled an old cowpoke, I was still moving upwards. Nothing was going to stop me getting up the mountain.

I greeted Steve with the words, 'Where's my horse?' And then resolutely passed him.

'God in heaven, Brian,' he said, 'you should go down.'

'No, Steve,' I responded defiantly. 'I'm all right. I've had a bit of a setback that's all. In half an hour I'll be myself again. I still feel fit and strong. Just stay with me and I'll get through this.'

He smiled and shook his head and we made our way up a snow slope. While I had been having trouble with my bowels, Stephen Wykes, the geophysicist, had decided that it was time for him to return to base camp. He was a kind, thoughtful young man, and we would miss him.

An hour later the sun came up and Steve and I came across the dead German in the snow. He looked for all the world like one of those chocolate soldiers that my mother used to hang on the Christmas tree when I was a lad. They were always covered in blue and silver paper. Steve and I were moved. It was a solemn occasion. I moved towards the unfortunate man and spoke these lines by Wordsworth:

My heart leaps up when I behold
A rainbow in the sky:
So was it when my life began;
So is it now I am a man;
So be it when I shall grow old,
Or let me die!
The Child is father of the Man;
And I could wish my days to be
Bound to each by natural piety.

William Wordsworth, 'My heart leaps up when I behold'

I looked up at the Stone Sentinel. It looked mysterious and dangerous. There we were, Steve and I, standing upon a cooled bed of ancient lava, and yet it was cold winds and altitude that was a our problem. We nodded to each other and continued to climb. Onward and upward, as the saying goes but the pain in my stomach was as bad as ever.

After a couple of hours we reached 21,000 feet (6,400 m) and caught up with the others. They were huddled together beneath a great rock wall. The wind was bad and the cold intense. From this position we had to follow a rough horizontal trail beneath a gigantic cliff which eventually led to a large ice couloir that plunged down from higher up the mountain. We had to cross this. Previous climbers had created a path through the ice but it was narrow and slippery. And it was alarmingly exposed. The couloir continued to plunge downwards to the right of the path at an angle of 40 degrees, for at least a mile or so. We all had ski sticks and an ice-axe.

A lot of the climbers were feeling the cold quite badly. I was very concerned when David Martin Jenkins suddenly sat down and asked Steve and Daniel, with some urgency, to warm his feet. The cold had got through in spite of his plastic boots. They pulled them off and placed his stocking feet in their crutches and armpits. After 10 minutes or so they gave them a long massage and once more placed them under their armpits. It worked, thank God! And David was once more on his feet.

Directly ahead of us was a long, arduous snow and ice field, which took us an hour and a half to ascend. After battling against the strong wind we crossed to the right and encountered another steep snow slope, the top of which led to the dreaded Canaletto, the crux of the climb. It was becoming a hell of a battle!

The canaletto is a gigantic pile of scree, littered with boulders of all shapes and sizes. It has neither form nor beauty. That great climber, Reinhold Messner says, 'The stone which I push up the mountain is my own psyche's.'

Well there are plenty of stones for psyches in the Canaletto. It was this formidable place in 1897 that burned off and defeated the man with the will of iron, the redoubtable English climber Edward Fitzgerald. And I could understand why. What I love about climbing mountains, apart from the friendships that are formed, is its rhythm. The delight of moving rhythmically upwards is almost ecstatic. This experience is denied the climber on the Canaletto and when you have a large amount of Immodium battling with rebel bacteria in your tummy, it's perfectly hideous. As I stared up at this 1,500 foot (457 m) of debris I could see the final summit ridge and the summit itself. But between 21,600 feet (6,661 m) and 22,830 feet (6,958 m) lay this ghastly obstacle.

For the next hour or so, my companions and I seemed to be making no progress at all. Every time I took a step up, I slid two steps down. My stomach cramps had me doubled over in pain. I tried everything in my power to alleviate this, using mind tricks of every description. It was a fruitless occupation and the spasms of pain persisted. For a long period I rested and groaned like a sexed-up moose. Everybody was getting ahead of me, except Steve, who hung around not knowing what to do to help. He just kept patting me on the back and saying,

'Not far Brian, not far!'

I smiled and tried not to laugh because it hurt so much.

'I'm just a bag of shit,' I whispered.

Suddenly Francisco was alongside me. He'd been there all the time, and I'd not seen him.

'We show thees mountain who is boss, eh Mister Brian? Bollocks eh? Let's rock 'n' roll!'

His kindness almost made me cry and gave me renewed strength.

'That's right Francisco,' I gasped. 'Bollocks! Let's rock 'n' roll.'

For the next half-hour I got quite a move on. Keeping to the right I found the scree a lot firmer. Yes, the ridge was getting closer! At times I bellowed in pain, but the X factor was beginning to kick in, and for the first time I realized I was going to make it.

'You've gotta want it.' That's what David Breashears had said to me. I was amused to hear John Beckett, the lawyer on our expedition, grumbling and swearing like a coal-miner. He was a loveable, dark-haired Scot, and he was castigating Ruth who was ahead of him and burrowing away like Squirrel Nutkin and causing stones to roll down into his path and hinder his progress.

> *There was naught to rouse their anger yet the*
> *Oath that each one swore*
> *Seemed less fit for publication*
> *Than the one that went before.*
>
> Henry Lawson, 'Bastard from the Bush'

I found myself laughing uncontrollably. The pain it caused was excruciating, but that didn't seem to matter. Steve started laughing too. It was a great shared moment of release.

I was just below the ridge now. I thanked Steve profusely for all his kindness and support. I heard shouting and screaming ahead of me. Elizabeth and Ruth were the first up. Lee Nobman and that grand man David Goode arrived next, followed by the rest. I still had a way to go and insisted that Francisco go ahead of me. I struggled for another fifteen minutes and was just 50 feet (15 m) from the top when Lee Nobman looked down and said, 'You are almost there Big Guy.'

I took a few steps to my left. There was a large cleft in the rock and would you believe it, a great dark condor flew out of it over my head.

'Did you see that?' I shouted.

'Yes,' said Elizabeth, smiling. 'This way Brian.'

Ten seconds later I was standing on the summit of the Stone Sentinel. Everyone embraced me. For a long time we held each other in a grip of happiness. A kind middle-aged Chilean gentleman, who had just led a Chilean expedition up the mountain, graciously presented me with the Chilean Monte Aconcagua Expedition flag. As I tied it on to my ice-axe he whispered conspiratorially, 'Your Prince Charles has been very naughty with Mrs Camilla-Parker Bowles.'

On the flight home, I found myself looking down and far away at the Brazilian jungles and for the first time in my life I could actually see the distant forests of the Matto Grosso that I had dreamed of for so many years. They went on and on for hundreds of miles. The sun had just set and a bright moon shone wonderfully in the high stratosphere. Down below sheet lightning lit up the dense dark clouds above the rain forests, and dazzling blue forked lightning revealed mysterious hidden valleys and rivers. The discharge ripped directly from billowing cumulonimbus cloud, the lower layers of which bore a preponderance of negatively charged water droplets to the positively charged earth. The result was a deluge of rain released from the huge cloud base. Drinking coffee from the safety of the plane, I was mesmerized by the power and scale of it all. It was as if the great mythical Toltec Dragon, Quetzalcoatl, was sending down radioactive rays of mass destruction. Gradually the plane moved away, and the vision faded into the dark cloak of night.

PART THREE

THE LOST WORLD

10

PROFESSOR CHALLENGER

On 9 October 1993, nine months after climbing Aconcagua, I reached 28,000 feet (8,534 m) on the south-east ridge of Everest, without the use of oxygen. It was also my 58th birthday. This was a Himalayan Kingdoms Expedition, led once more by Steve Bell. It successfully placed sixteen of its team on the summit. Steve, of course being one of them. Ramon Blanco, the Venezuelan climber, was on the expedition and at the tender age of 60 became the oldest man to climb Everest. A stunning achievement. The news of Ramon's success sent shockwaves across the Himalayas. A truly amazing man.

You can see where I am leading, can't you? Ramon, Venezuela, the Lost World. Over a good many years he had explored vast areas of the Gran Sabana. The Lost World was his pride and joy and he had once taken Steve Bell there.

'You really must go there, Brian,' said Ramon at base camp one evening.

'Oh yes,' I sighed, 'I am dying to go.'

After Ramon had summited and returned to base camp, I took it on myself to look after him and to get him down the valleys to Lukla, where small twin-engined planes ferried people back to Kathmandu. He was cold and exhausted and on the journey down he kept saying to me, over and over again, 'I am dead! I have no brain, I'm brain-dead.'

'Nonsense!' I said, and pinched his cheeks to prove to him that he would be fine. He smiled and whispered, 'You must come with me to the Lost World, Brian, it's so warm there.'

Inevitably I lost touch with Ramon, when I returned home to pick up my life and my career again and so years passed and life went on its merry way.

During the second week in April 1998 I went for a long enjoyable run around Chobham Common with all of the dogs. They loved it. As I panted and sweated they ran and swam in every pond and lake they could find. After the run I bundled them into my tough, old beaten-up Nissan Prairie. There they lay, happy, breathless and covered in mud and filth. Mind you I didn't look much better myself. It meant that I would have to shower them down with the hose before allowing them into the house. After twenty minutes I arrived home and let the 'muck-lumps' out. I was just about to open the gate and turn on the tap when the postman arrived in his red van. I immediately burst into song, '"The postman rides over village and moor, with letters for the rich and poor." Good news I hope, Simon,' I said laughing, 'Don't give me any bills, I've got no money.'

'No bills I promise,' he replied, smiling.

Simon was about 28 years old, tall, good-looking with tight wavy hair and in spite of being a shy lad he was always keen to talk to me about expeditions. Twice a week for a few minutes I would whet his appetite with stories of epic adventures and leave him begging for more. On this occasion he wanted to know about the dreaded ice fall above the Khumbu Glacier on Everest's south side. He was spellbound as I described to him how I had ascended it five times in 1993. He shook his head in disbelief and said, 'Mr Blessed, I could never do anything like that.'

'Nonsense,' I replied, 'there's nothing in this world you can't do if you set your mind to it.' He paused a while and, after looking downwards, said meekly, 'Well, the only thing I've done is to go to Roraima in Venezuela last year, but it doesn't compare to Mount Everest.'

Time stood still, the birds stopped singing, newts stopped copulating, frogs lost their ability to 'brevit', my filthy dogs ceased panting and became statues. After a long McCready pause, I whispered in the tiniest voice in creation, 'You went where?'

'To Roraima,' he repeated. 'It's in Venezuela. Some people call it the Lost World.'

'I thought that's what you said.' I gripped him by the shoulders.

'How? Where? Who? What? Impossible! You've been where? This is mad! It's crazy! You can't have been to the Lost World! No! This is ridiculous! How in God's name, Simon, did you manage to get there?'

'Oh,' he said mildly, 'I read about it in a brochure from a company called Explore. They're based in Aldershot and organize treks all over the world. One of their expeditions goes to Roraima, but I don't think you would want to do that. You go on hard climbs on the highest mountains.'

'Not want to go! I've been dying to go there since I stopped wearing nappies. When can you bring me the brochure?' I asked with some urgency.

'Tomorrow,' he replied smiling.

The boot was on the other foot now and I was the one who was begging for more. 'I'll have to go, Mr Blessed, I'm late,' he explained and off he went down the lane, leaving me covered in dust, confounded and impatient. I was poleaxed.

'God,' I said out loud, 'I just don't believe this. My postman is delivering the Lost World in the morning via a company twenty minutes down the road in Aldershot.'

My five mucky dogs cocked their heads on one side and tried to understand the very peculiar behaviour of their biped master. As I washed them down I sang a song from my childhood,

> *'You'll find that happiness lies, right under*
> *Your eyes,*
> *Back in your own back yard.'*

It really was ridiculously funny. From the earliest days of my childhood I have longed to reach the Lost World. Journeys all over the world had taken me to deserts, volcanoes, glaciers, snow fields, jungles, even up the mighty ridges of Everest itself. Still I had not found my way to Roraima, and now, on my very own doorstep, the keys of the kingdom were about to be handed over to me by 'Postman Pat'! As an American Polar explorer said to me recently in Resolute, Canada, 'Isn't that the darndest thing?'

The following morning I placed a garden chair beside our wooden postbox and sat there waiting impatiently like a little boy, with my furry four-legged friends beside me. I sang happily,

> *'I'll be waitin' where the lane begins,*
> *Waitin' for you, all needles and pins.*
> *Til then, the world is gonna be mine*
> *Mine all mine, this mornin', about a*
> *Quarter to nine.'*

Down the rough unmade road that leads to our cottage came 'Postman Pat' in his red van. Out he popped and, grinning from ear to ear, presented me with a couple of tatty pages.

'Where's the brochure, Simon?' I inquired, somewhat disappointed.

'Oh, I'm afraid this is all I've got left of it. But these two pages do tell you about the expedition and has the address of the company on the back.'

I laughed and thanked him profusely and we talked for a few minutes about Venezuela. Then I gave him a Himalayan Kingdoms brochure with information about treks to Everest Base Camp and we said 'Cheerio'. Five minutes later I was on the phone to Explore in Aldershot. Five days later I was accepted on an expedition to the Lost World, which was due to depart on 29 June and return on 20 July.

Though it was only 22 days a lot would be packed into it. I reread Sir Arthur Conan Doyle's novel and kept repeating joyfully to myself, 'I'm going to the Lost World!'

Before going on any expedition, I always carry out a simple ritual.

There is a hill overlooking Chobham Common near my home. I always make a pilgrimage to this spot. People fly model aircraft here and it is an oasis of calm and relaxation for them. Here I lie on my back after my obligatory run and ruminate about the delights that await me on my next venture, in this case the Lost World.

As my dogs nestled around me and I listened to the buzz of the toy planes some words of Eric Shipton's came to mind,

The springs of enchantment lie within ourselves;
They arise from our sense of wonder, that most
Precious of gifts, the birth right of every child.

'That Untravelled World'

Anthony Rivas Merrill, the expedition leader, lived in Venezuela and would meet us at Caracas Airport. Our party, including Anthony, numbered ten plus the Indians who would be helping us. It was, therefore, a fair-sized expedition. We assembled at the check-in area of British Midland at Heathrow for the flight to Frankfurt, where we would change to Avianca Airlines and fly on to Caracas.

The other members of the expedition looked young and fit and cheerful. They welcomed me with open arms and made me feel one of them even though I was old enough to be their father, possibly even their grandfather.

As far as I could ascertain there were three married couples and two young, very eligible bachelors. Someone asked,

'Hey Brian, why are you going to Venezuela?'

'To find some dinosaurs,' I shouted. 'I want to catch some iguanodons, and take them on *The Big Breakfast* show. They don't eat much, I think they eat turnips.'

'We'll help you find them,' said Nick Moss, a tall handsome fellow who was busy supervising everyone's luggage.

'By the way, Brian, this is my wife Marianne. Everyone calls her Maz.'

'Then I'll call her Maz too,' I said. 'Nice to meet you.'

Maz was about 5 feet 6 inches (1.7 m), with lovely blonde hair. She flashed me a winning smile and inquired about what jabs I had had, as she was not sure she had had all of the ones required.

'The BBC Medical Officer, from The Natural History Unit in Bristol, has kindly administered most of them for me,' I replied. 'They are the basic jabs that everyone has to have really: cholera, yellow fever, chagas disease, T.B., hepatitis B, meningitis and the main vaccinations against paralytic rabies, which is transmitted by the evil vampire bat which lives and multiplies by sucking blood from herbivorous animals and humans. There are three species of these creatures of the night: the common vampire bat, the hairy legged vampire bat and the white spotted vampire bat, though the latter is not so important from a disease angle as the other two.'

Maz's mouth had opened as wide as the black hole of Calcutta.

'Not to worry, Maz,' I continued. 'It is reported (presumably by those who later died) that the vampire has a soporific effect on its victim, and that the one consolation is, that you don't feel the bite unless it is infected.'

'Oh, my God!' Maz cried out.

'You'll be all right, Maz, as long as you have the vaccine. I've been protected by the "200th Duck Egg Passaged Flury Strain Modified Live Virus Vaccine" which is injected through the tummy. If you've not had it and get bitten by the hairy legged vampire bat, then by the time you get the vaccine in Caracas, you could end up hanging upside-down from the nearest tree!'

'I'm going to get even with you, Brian Blessed,' Maz said laughing. 'Just you wait.'

By now, Nick had gathered up all our tickets and passports and presented them at the check-in desk. Our luggage passed speedily through and two hours later we were on board our flight bound for Frankfurt. When we arrived in Frankfurt we had a two-hour wait before our onward flight to Caracas. My young companions took it upon themselves to nag and look after me.

'Come on Brian, where's your passport? Where's your form? The gentleman is waiting.'

The gentleman in question was a 40-year-old German with eyes as cold as the Arctic frost and he was in no mood for comedians!

'Ver iss your yellow pass?' he said. 'I cannot let you through unless you have ze pass.'

After a great deal of scrutiny by all and sundry, it was discovered stuck to the back of my airline ticket by a gentle, quiet spoken man called David Gardiner. After a great deal of deliberation, the Prussian Ice Warrior let us through and we were on our way to one of the most spectacular, sensual and easygoing countries in the whole of Latin America – Venezuela. Yes, I was finally on my way. I slipped off my trainers, and settled back into my seat grinning like a Cheshire Cat.

'Seen any dinosaurs, Brian?' said Nick, who was seated two rows in front of me. 'Yes,' I said. 'It's funny that you should ask that, I've just seen a pterodactyl fly past my window with an oxygen mask on.'

'Oh, bad form,' responded Nick. 'Not like you on Everest, eh, Brian? That's cheating, using oxygen.'

'Oh by the way, I hope Maz has remembered to pack a thick stick for the expedition.'

'Why's that?' Maz asked, sipping an orange juice.

'Snakes, Maz, snakes. There's a rattlesnake that lives in the jungles around Roraima which is normally referred to as the grass snake, so use a thick walking stick to thump the ground as vibration upsets it and it runs away.'

'Oh, my God!' Maz groaned, and we all giggled.

Maz and the other two ladies, Janet and Karen, were smashing girls. Over the years, it would be fair to say that I have found a great many men disappointing. Not always, of course, but sometimes. The ladies on the other hand are usually a joy and an inspiration, full of common sense and wisdom.

They were a terrific group of youngsters, but I was aware that a certain amount of diplomacy on my part would not come amiss. I wanted to film my adventure on a digital video camera, without intruding on their privacy. They had all paid a considerable sum of money to be on the expedition and the prospect of reaching and exploring the Lost World meant just as much to them as it did to me.

In the final analysis they instinctively trusted me and I was grateful for their generosity of spirit.

The plane touched down in Caracas at 5.00 p.m. on 29 June. Weirdly enough we all shook hands, as if welcoming each other to Venezuela. It was wonderful! And why shouldn't we have been excited? This expedition by small bus, four-wheel drive vehicles, motorized canoe, light aircraft and on foot, reached deep into territory almost unknown to the rest of the world.

The heat hit me as we disembarked from the plane. I'd never experienced anything like it, not even in Jamaica. The air was moist and sticky and in next to no time I was bathed in sweat. It didn't improve inside the terminal building, in fact it was probably worse.

Our flight was slightly early and our luggage came through quickly. Consequently we found that we were there before Anthony, our leader.

'Don't worry,' said Janet Butterworth, 'Explore won't let us down, they are a very reliable company. We went with them last year to Machu Picchu and Lake Titicaca in Peru and it was a wonderfully organized trip.'

Five minutes after Janet's reassurance, our leader, Anthony Rivas Merrill made his appearance. I have written a great deal about this man at the beginning of the book, and I shall write a great deal more about him before it is finished. Suffice to say, that from the moment he introduced himself and meticulously checked all our belongings, he was outstanding in every respect. What also endeared him to me was that he likened me in appearance to Conan Doyle's Professor Challenger, and called me by that name from that moment on.

He led us out of the terminal to a private bus parked nearby that would take us to the Hotel Guacharo. The driver you are familiar with, for it was the flamboyant character Silva who was to become our 'bosom' companion. The bus pulled out of the terminal, edged past decrepit trucks carrying all manner of goods, and headed on to a new six-lane highway which took us eventually to our neat little hotel.

After dinner I decided to sit on the flat roof of the hotel, which was by now deserted, and 'take coffee'. From there I had a great view of the city lights and the skyline. In eight days' time we would be approaching the intimidating cliffs of Roraima. I pulled out a crumpled piece of paper from my pocket containing the words of Sir Robert Schomburgk, who in 1838 had reached the base of the elevated plateau after an arduous trek lasting several months:

Before sunrise and half an hour after, Roraima was beautifully clear, which enabled us to see it in all its grandeur. Those stupendous walks rise to a height of 1,500 feet. They are perpendicular as if erected with a plumb-line; nevertheless in some parts they are overhung with low shrubs which, seen from a distance, give a dark hue to the reddish rock. Baron Von Humboldt observed that a rock of 1,600 feet of perpendicular height has been sought for in vain in the Swiss Alps, nor do I think that Guina offers another example of that description. A much more remarkable feature of this locality, however, lies in the cascades, which fall from their enormous height, and, strange as it may appear, afterwards flow in different directions into three of the mightiest rivers of the northern half of South America, namely the Amazon, the Orinoco, and the Essequibo. For these wonderful cascades Roraima is famed among the Indians who in their dances sing of the wonder of 'Roraima', the red rock, wrapped in clouds, the ever fertile source of the streams. I can imperfectly describe the magnificent appearance of these mountains. They convey the idea of vast buildings and might be called 'Nature's Forum'.

'British Government Survey of 1834'

Bright and early the following morning we loaded our gear on to Silva's shining white bus and we were ready for the off. As the chorus in Shakespeare's *Henry V* (Act II, Chorus 1) says,

> *Now all the youth of England are on fire,*
> *And silken dalliance in the wardrobe lies; . . .*
> *. . . For now sits Expectation in the air*

'To the Lost World', they all shouted, as we set off.

I sat alongside the grinning Silva. '*Musica!*' he roared, switching on the radio which blasted out some popular Venezuelan music. On and off went my video camera as the panorama of Caracas unveiled itself. What chaos! Cars reversed from side streets directly in front of the bus, not to mention the handcarts, and a variety of animals!

Anthony stood alongside me looking smart in a blue shirt and matching shorts. He gave a running commentary as I filmed and the sound and energy of the bustling city hit us from all sides. The bus began to climb and all manner of skyscrapers came into view. Beneath them, the hillsides were covered in dismal shanty towns. 'Look closely, Professor Challenger,' said Anthony, 'and you will see that from almost every tin roof there protrudes a TV aerial. The poverty of the shanty towns contrasts weirdly with the almost intimidating array of glass sky-scrapers and modern kinetic sculptures, and you will notice that the side streets are filled with impoverished vendors selling cheap American music tapes and T-shirts with messages in English. So "Welcome to Venezuela", Challenger!'

Silva now steered the bus into a quiet, rich quarter of the city sporting luxurious white and yellow buildings surrounded by magnificent walled gardens. There were masses of trees everywhere. In a short space of time we ascended a steep imposing highway and stopped at the top. From there we had wonderful panoramic views of Caracas.

'This is called the Highway of 1,000 Metres,' said Anthony, as I stepped off the bus to film the view. He stood alongside me and continued to talk, 'The wealthy Caracas, of glass and concrete, was built mostly in the 1970s at the peak of the petroleum boom, when the price of crude oil quadrupled overnight and the country was dubbed "Saudi Venezuela" by its envious neighbours. Its alter ego, the impoverished Caracas that exists alongside, is a legacy of the oil crash of the 1980s. Yet rich or poor, in the 1990s it has become a Caribbean city where the bulk of the population under twenty years of age is addicted to baseball, fast food and soap operas.'

'Thank you, Anthony,' I said, turning off my camera and mounting the steps of the bus again, 'you should be on television.'

'Oh no!' he replied shyly, 'I will leave that to you, Challenger.'

'How's your filming going, Brian?' said Maz, smiling.

'Oh fine, thanks Maz. Anthony was just telling me about the kaboura fly which is even smaller than the West Highland midge from Scotland, and decidedly more vicious. Your skin rises in multiple pimples which take about six weeks to subside.'

'Oh, my God!' groaned Maz.

'It's all right, Maz,' said Anthony, laughing. 'They are only found in the vicinity of water, which is a relief.'

A short while later the bus went through a long tunnel that cut through the surrounding mountains. Anthony said that it was one of the most expensive tunnels ever built. It was a ghastly experience! It went on for miles and the fumes from the vehicles were horrendous. We all held our breath and put our shirts over our noses, but to no avail. The deadly carbon monoxide penetrated our defences. When we came out on the other side we were all gasping for breath. The bus entered a green valley surrounded by high wooded trees. We let out a sigh of relief and felt much happier.

We stopped soon after outside a large shop which sold everything from camping accessories to whisky and guns. I had never seen so many guns, any gun you wanted you could buy.

'Come on, Challenger,' said Anthony, pointing to a particularly vicious-looking Kalashnikov. 'Buy this, then you can shoot yourself a Tyrannosaurus rex like the one in *Jurassic Park*.'

The amount of whisky for sale was incredible, every brand you could think of. The Scots apparently make it especially for Venezuelans, as they drink more whisky than any other nation.

With delighted incredulity, I observed the football World Cup on a TV screen in the shop. We were able to follow the competition throughout the trip.

Once more we were on the bus heading eastwards towards our destination of Mochima, which was situated on the Caribbean coast some six hours' drive away. Silva really started to motor now and the scenery was breathtaking, with miles and miles of jungle on either side of the road.

The bus was well stocked with soft drinks and fruit, so we wanted for nothing. We stopped once more for a short break and for the first time noticed the gentle humming of the insects. A few yellow butterflies appeared, and I heard the distinctive droning of a bumble bee of which there are many species in South America. The green carpet of plants surrounding the masses of trees stretched as far as the eye could see and the gentle rhythmic sounds of the jungle caressed my heart and mind. I longed to explore those green mansions. I basked in the sun and the warm rain and I found myself humming a tune from my infant school days,

> '*After the sun, the rain,*
> *After the rain, the sun.*
> *This is how it's always bin,*
> *Since the Earth begun.*'

Kukenan, looking so beautiful from the summit of Roraima.
How sad that it is called 'suicide mountain'.

One of the many *tepui*s of Venezuela, as seen
from an aeroplane. An 'island in the sky'.

Quartz crystal found in the crystal lake.

Swimming in the crystal lake.

The entrance to 'The Pit'.

Naked swimmer in the crystal lake at the base of 'The Pit'.

Devil's Canyon from the air.

Happy at the thought of entering Devil's Canyon.

Kavak Gorge, the entrance to
Devil's Canyon.

Kavak Falls in the heart of Devil's Canyon.

Our departure for Angel Falls, along Carrao River.

View of Carrao River from our boat.

Wei Tepui, seen from Carrao River.

Fauna and flora of the rainforest on the banks of the Carrao River: tree frog.

Vine snake.

Ocelot.

White heron.

Howler monkey.

Iguana.

Twenty-four-hour ant.

Orchid.

Wild rhubarb.

Bromeliad.

Angel Falls.

Nick at the base of Angel Falls.

A wrecked Dakota which we discovered during a short
expedition from the boat on the way to Canaima.

Our final destination, Canaima Lagoon.

Our aeroplane, crashed in the neighbourhood of Lagartijo Reservoir in the Tuy Valley.

My Jack Russell, Duke, 'He Who Must Be Obeyed'.
Seeing one just like him in the Indian village gave me quite a shock.

As Boss Nass, King of the Gunguns.

Half an hour later we came to a little stall at the side of the road selling Indian bread, which Anthony informed me contained 99 per cent fibre and lots of molasses. 'Keeps you regular,' he laughed.

It was absolutely delicious, and so was the coconut drink that Silva kindly supplied me with.

'This is gorgeous!' I yelled. 'This journey can go on forever, as far as I am concerned. You could run right round the moon and it wouldn't be as good as this!'

Andrew Bawn joined me. He was about 6 feet (1.8 m) tall and came from Falkirk – the only Scotsman in our party. It was obvious that he would have to be very careful with the sun, for he had very fair skin. Surprisingly, for a man in his early 20s, he had very little hair, but it suited him and we all said so, which delighted him. Come to think of it, he was always delighted about something. He was very clever, worked for BP, and had a great passion for swimming.

Our journey now took us through the state of Barcelona which is a major source of petroleum and is one of the largest producers of oil in the country. Barcelona is the capital of the state and the site of an airport which also serves the town of Puerto La Paz. Between Barcelona and Puerto La Paz is the turning to the mammoth tourist complex and the beaches of El Morro. We avoided this, thank goodness, and travelled along the final stretch of coastal highway towards our destination. The journey between Puerto La Cruz and Mochima is aptly referred to as the 'Route Of The Sun', and is one of the most picturesque coastal roads in the country. The steep winding highway is cut into the sides and along the base of mountains that plunge dramatically into the sea. Around each curve we were presented with yet another beautiful vista of rugged coastline and pounding waves. Here, there and everywhere were delightful coves, harbouring beaches rimmed with palm trees.

At about 4 o'clock in the afternoon we approached the turn off for the fishing village of Mochima. We had arrived. Our tiny, rustic hotel was called Basilio, and it was lapped by the Caribbean. The staff were very laid back and friendly and we felt at home at once. The dining area was a large comfortable verandah with a quaint red roof that looked out over the Bay of Mochima. The Bay gives its name to the National Park and at 3.5 miles (5.5 km) across, is one of the finest sheltered harbours in Venezuela. This was just what the doctor ordered, and, joy of joys, we were going to stay here for three days. We couldn't believe our luck.

We took our time unpacking and made our way to the verandah where coffee and soft drinks were served. Afterwards we climbed up a road just outside the village and reached a place called Cerro Aceite Castillo where we found spectacular views of the islands of the Mochima National Park. That evening we sampled the traditional fish dishes in one of the local restaurants and then returned to the comfort of the hotel verandah where we proceeded to sip milky coffee in a leisurely fashion.

The tropical night had a billion eyes and two hours later the members of the Lost World expedition closed theirs, and slept.

'You must wear factor 15 at least, or you will burn badly in this sun.' It was morning and Anthony was advising us about the use of sun cream. 'The sun here is very hot. We are going to be swimming and snorkelling for three days. The purpose of this stay is to acclimatize you for the ascent of Roraima. You need to acclimatize gradually and to get used to the heat, but you must not get burnt. In a few days you will be carrying rucksacks and you don't want them rubbing against sore skin.'

We boarded a local launch to explore the offshore islands, and to spend the rest of the day on one of them, where lunch would be served and we would swim and snorkel all day. The ever-faithful Silva came with us and he never stopped smiling and watching like a hawk. Every time he sensed I was thirsty, he would produce a soft drink from nowhere, like Paul Daniels! It was magic!

Our pretty launch was shaded with a white canopy, and as it cut through the water we were hit by the spray. It was delightful. I filmed it all, and Anthony was once more the star of the show. He pointed to a small island and said, 'There are semi-wild goats living there. They are known to drink seawater but do not become dehydrated. As rainwater is scarce on the island they combine it with seawater. The minerals in the rainwater filter out the salt and the goats survive. It is said that humans can do this when they are adrift at sea. The secret is not to allow themselves to become too thirsty. While they are still unthirsty they must drink a little seawater and the body will use its own fluid to filter out the salt.'

A few minutes later we landed on a wonderful white sandy beach with coconut trees as a backdrop.

It was quite simply paradise. There wasn't a soul in sight. White brick huts with sugar-cane roofs were dotted here and there, deck-chairs and parasols were stored inside and the two cheerful Pemon Indians who had brought us over set about erecting them. Our picnic lunches had been kept cool in ice boxes aboard the launch. Presto, pronto, everything was set up and we were in business. Everybody charged into the sea and became water-babies. I resisted the temptation to follow as I wanted to do some filming.

'Watch out for barracuda, Maz,' I shouted as she porposied about with her hubby, Nick.

And back came the guaranteed response, 'Oh my God! There are no barracuda here, are there Anthony?'

'No,' he answered. 'They usually stay far out at sea.'

'Why are you here, Janet?' I inquired.

'Because I want to see the Lost World,' she said. Her ready smile always put me at ease. 'And you Miles?' I asked her husband. 'Same as Janet,' he said, splashing her face.

David Gardiner, a quiet fair-headed lad, was nursing a sore shoulder, and therefore sensibly made himself comfortable on a deck-chair.

I soon got fed up with filming and joined the others in the water. My swimming resembles that of a walrus, I'm told. I'm strong, but slow, and I splash a lot.

Anthony and the Pemon Indians, assisted by Silva, made our lunch, which was bloody scrumptious. We ate all kinds of lovely fish and mouth-watering vegetables, and then snoozed and swam, swam and snoozed.

11

TO THE GRAN SABANA

For the next few days Anthony took us to different islands where we swam and snorkelled, ate wonderful lunches, snoozed and swam, and swam and snoozed. God it was tough! But after three days we were getting brown and acclimatized and we waved a very reluctant goodbye to Mochima and got back on the bus.

After half an hour we stopped by a stall on the roadside which sold traditional black-faced rag dolls, amongst other things. What interested me were the hand-carved replica sailboats. Another stall was full of hundreds of stuffed piranha fish. There were boxes in corners full of them. It was distressing to see a badly stuffed ocelot. These beautiful cats are supposed to be protected, though I am glad to say that this was the only one I saw.

One and a half hours after leaving Mochima, we reached Cumana which lies in another very beautiful bay. Cumana, nicknamed 'First Born of the Continent', was the first Spanish settlement on the South American continent, established by Franciscan friars in 1515. Cumanagoto Indians mounted many devastating assaults on the town, although, of course, Indian resistance was quite understandable. The Spaniards enslaved them and used their labour to harvest pearls from the rich seabed. We left this fascinating town and turned inland towards Caripe and eventually the Orinoco river.

Half-way to Caripe, Anthony gave us a choice, we could push on over the Orinoco and press on to our night stop at Upata, or take a shorter journey and stay at Caripe and have the wonderful bonus of visiting the famous Guacharo Caves. We chose the latter as we could easily make up the lost time the next day. These famous caves were first visited by Baron von Humboldt in 1799. It was at this time that he heard of 'The Mine Of Fat'. It seemed an extraordinary name for a cave.

He was told that it was the home of the Guacharo – the 'Night Bird'. Guides led them to the great cave and they carried their torches high above their heads. Yellow light fell on to the damp floor and cast great shadows up the walls.

What strange vegetation sprouted in this forgotten darkness! [wrote Humboldt]. *Seed dropped by the so-called Night Birds, had germinated in the mould covering the rocks and the form and colour of the plants had been changed beyond all recognition! Darkness is everywhere connected with death. The Grotto of Caripe is the Tartarus of the Greeks. And the* Guacharos *which hover over the rivulet uttering plaintive cries, reminded one of the Stygian birds. The natives, restrained by their superstitions, refused to penetrate further into the cave.*
The Voyages of Humboldt and Bonpland

Bonpland, Humboldt's partner, fired his gun into the darkness above them, killing one of the birds. Humbolt picked it up and opened its abdomen with a knife.

We found the Guacharo *– or oil bird – up to this time a genus of bird thought to be merely legendary by students of zoology. Their peritoneum is loaded with fat which reaches from the abdomen to the anus, forming a kind of cushion between the legs.*

When we arrived in the vicinity of Caripe, Silva parked his bus in a tiny, picturesque car park. I was so excited I could hardly hold my camera. How peaceful the area was. It was about 3.00 p.m. and the green gorge glistened with the softness of newly fallen rain. I veered my camera from right to left and focused on the impressive limestone cliffs above the gigantic entrance to the cave. It was a staggering sight. I could understand now why von Humboldt was so fascinated by it, and why he described the cave as the 'Tartarus of the Greeks', for it reminded me of the cave at Delphi in Greece. Water gently cascaded down tiny hidden waterfalls and birds and insects combined to give a delicate background hum. Suddenly, I heard the noisy chatter of some parakeets and saw several of them flying across the gorge, their brilliant green plumage flashing in the afternoon sun. Then peace once again. As yet none of us could hear any oil birds.

Our guide was a young Venezuelan lady called Rosa. Rosa lit a gas lamp and led our party along a meandering pathway towards the entrance of the cave.

Ferns of all description adorned the footpath and dotted amongst them were trumpet flowers (which I believe have psychedelic properties) and passion flowers, whose stems and tendrils reached into every nook and cranny. The abundance of insects, flowers and seed attracted a remarkable number of hummingbirds. It was all so seductive that I found myself lagging behind and had to hurry to catch up.

Rosa and my companions were now inside the entrance, her bright yellow light was surrounded by a strange darkness. Now at last I could hear the legendary oil birds. It was the most eerie sound I have ever heard. Once I caught up with the party, Rosa lifted her lamp to reveal a weird landscape as I had only seen in nightmares. A landscape full of demons, witches, hobgoblins and long-lost souls. Life adapts itself to all conditions and there was life everywhere. The damp, black floor beneath our feet was crawling with thousands of black and red millipedes. In the darkness I could feel spiders' webs brushing my face and I thought, Madame Tussauds has nothing on this, for this was a real Chamber of Horrors. And I loved it. It was absolutely astonishing.

Just inside the entrance the cave was huge, the roof seemed to go on for ever, disappearing into a gloomy nothingness. Small lakes and ponds were revealed by the light and you had to watch your footing. The rocks looked as if they were covered in masses of wax. They were macabrely unattractive, as if a legion of sick dragons had vomited down them for centuries, and the vomit had congealed and solidified into representations of the dragons' souls.

Every movement of Rosa's friendly yellow lamp revealed a never-ending gallery of crystallized, grotesque monsters. The lamp became the centre of the universe. I moved ahead of everybody to get a better angle of the approaching party and the entrance of the cave, from this point, looked wonderfully bright against the severe black background. The deeper we went the smaller the entrance looked, until it finally disappeared.

But, my readers, what was truly astonishing was the sound of the hidden oil birds. There must have been thousands of them, hiding in the darkness above our heads, playing 'merry-pop'! I was thunderstruck! Never, in all my born days have I experienced anything like it. God it was exciting! I was out of my skull with happiness. This, for me, was 'Boys' Own' stuff, real adventure. Isn't it amazing where some creatures choose to live? The noise was deafening, but it made me laugh, the birds must have been furious with us, they were probably trying to get some sleep. Apparently they fly out of the cave at night to feed on the fruits of the nearby palm trees.

I could relate these marvellous raucous birds to Sir Arthur Conan Doyle's pterodactyls in *The Lost World*. Unable to contain myself I expounded on the theme to my gob-smacked companions. The oil birds' screeching chatter conveyed to me what masses of pterodactyls must have sounded like. Here's the extract from Doyle's novel:

Creeping to his side, we looked over the rocks. The place into which we gazed was a pit, and may, in the early days, have been one of the smaller volcanic blowholes of the plateau. It was bowl-shaped, and at the bottom, some hundreds of yards from where we lay, were pools of green-scummed, stagnant water, fringed with bulrushes. It was a weird place in itself, but its occupants made it seem like a scene from the Seven Circles of Dante. The place was a rookery of pterodactyls. There were hundreds of them congregated within view. All the bottom area round the water-edge was alive with their young ones, and with hideous mothers brooding upon their leathery, yellowish eggs. From this crawling flapping mass of obscene reptilian life came the shocking clamour which filled the air and the mephitic, horrible, musty odour which turned us sick. But above, perched each upon its own stone, tall, grey, and withered, more like dead and dried specimens than actual living creatures, sat the horrible males, absolutely motionless save for the rolling of their red eyes or an occasional snap of their rat-trap beaks as a dragonfly went past them. Their huge membranous wings were closed by folding their forearms, so that they sat like gigantic old women, wrapped in hideous web-coloured shawls, and with their ferocious heads protruding above them. Large and small, not less than a thousand of these filthy creatures lay in the hollow before us.

Well I don't have any pterodactyls to tell you about but I do have my oil birds.

Deeper inside the cave we came across a baby oil bird which had fallen out of its nest. Anthony told us that its fate was sealed, as hundreds of rats live on the floor of the cave, and they depend on such mishaps to restock their larder and, he told us, chicks fall out of their nests quite regularly. No sooner had he finished speaking then we saw a rat. We also saw an albino catfish and many kinds of spiders. The oil bird was hunted by the local Indians. They squeezed their abdomens to get at the oil and fat, which they used for their lamps and for cooking. The oil bird is the only bird to fly using sonar, like a bat.

As you can imagine the smell of ammonia in the cave was something else! The droppings on the floor are full of the seeds of palm trees, which sprout and grow everywhere, although they are somewhat stunted. Anthony told us that stalagmites and stalactites in the cave grow 1 inch (2.5 cm) every hundred years or so. Rosa showed us one 59 feet (18 m) high.

At 1,548 feet (472 m) the last rays of light disappear from the cave and this is as far as von Humboldt got. There is a plaque to honour his achievement. Unfortunately, the natives with him would go no further, believing that the souls of their ancestors were in the deep recesses of the cave and that the plants were phantoms, banished from the face of the Earth!

'Do you believe that, Rosa?' I asked. She nodded.

'Oh yes,' said Anthony. 'If we go any deeper we will be trespassing on ancestral burial grounds and the spirits could grab us and we could be lost for ever. But today, just for you Challenger, the gods will let us go on.'

After about 80 feet (24 m) we came to a large rock called the Religious Rock. It seems to be a mother and baby, grandfather, other members of a family and a dog. Rather lovely, I thought. We pressed on a little deeper. There were few oil birds here, maybe the spirits of their ancestors kept them away.

'The cave goes on and on,' said Anthony, 'I don't think it has ever been fully explored. And we don't have time to do it now. We have to go back.'

I lingered for a while filming the retreating lamp, then I suddenly found myself in darkness as Rosa disappeared around a corner.

And then, as I proceed, see his last light,
Die to a dark that would be night indeed:
Night where my soul might sail a million years
In nothing, not even death, not even tears.

John Masefield, 'Lollington Downs'

These words of John Masefield came to me and I hurried after the others and once more incurred the wrath of the harpies above me. Once outside, we all thanked Rosa and Anthony. It had been a sensational adventure.

As our visit had not taken up too much time, Anthony suggested that we head straight for Upata. We all agreed, as this would put us back on schedule.

Silva drove like a demon. It was raining and the forests were replaced by a vast vista of flat prairie land. Four hours later we hit a dreadful traffic jam, a gridlock for miles right in the middle of Venezuela. We couldn't believe it. To keep our spirits up we sang lots of songs like a proper coach party, and, of course, we always had Silva's *musica*! Slowly but surely the roads cleared and our lusty driver once again got some training for the Brazilian Grand Prix. The jungles appeared again and I found myself getting excited, and I urged Silva on, 'On, on you noblest Venezuelan, and gentleman in England now abed, shall think themselves acurst they were not here.'

'Yahoo, yahoo,' I raved. 'Lost World, here we come.'

I drummed a beat on the dashboard in front of me and murmured in a deep voice, 'We will kill you, if we can. We will kill you, if we can . . . Recognize it, Anthony?'

'No,' he smiled shaking his head and laughing at my insanity.

'It's from *The Lost World*. The heroes hear menacing "talk drums" up the river as they enter unknown territory. I believe that the unfriendly Indians who beat those drums were the invisible Bravos. We will kill you if we can. We will kill you if we can.'

Anthony laughed.

'Well, Challenger, the Indians we will meet in Roraima are called Pemon, and they are very visible and very friendly.'

Some hours later we reached the Orinoco. For the first time in my life I set eyes on this great river . . . and lo and behold it was night! The time that we had spent at the oil bird cave had cost a daytime view of the river. But weighing the pros and cons, it was well worth the sacrifice.

We crossed the mighty Orinoco and reached the town of Upata. The following day we would be entering the Gran Sabana.

We were all up at about 6.00 a.m. the next morning so that we would be ready to depart at 7.00 a.m. The Gran Sabana! Mouthwatering stuff. Then all hell broke loose! I received a fax from my agent saying that Luc Besson wanted me to start in five days' time on his film *Joan*, which was about Joan of Arc. Besson is renowned for being a remarkable film director and most actors would give their eye-teeth to work for him. The engagement, if I took it, would require my services for five months. All very tempting. I found myself in an appalling dilemma. I managed to get hold of my agent, Derek Webster, who told me that it was not a firm offer, but he was almost certain that Besson wanted me to play the part.

Talk about bloody wobbling! No one seemed to know what part it was. Besson is brilliant, but scripts, where he is concerned, are about as rare as the yeti! The casting director said it was 'a lovely part', but she couldn't guarantee that I would be offered it. If I returned from the expedition promptly there was a good chance that I would get the job. I gathered, from Derek, that filming this part would not start for another two months, but they needed to film one day of it to accommodate Faye Dunaway. Just a minute, I thought, give up a miraculous expedition, a childhood dream, because of a day's filming with Faye Dunaway? And if I managed to get back home, there was half a chance that I wouldn't get the part anyway!

The whole drama had taken up two hours of my time. I had spent a large amount of money on phone calls and now the expedition was late in setting off. The group had been so patient, and fully understood my predicament. In the end my agent and I agreed that it would be madness for me to return home. I thanked Derek for his trouble and hung up. I turned round and looked at Anthony and the team and said, 'Bollocks! I'm off to the Lost World.'

This was greeted with a hearty cheer.

I was absolutely gutted when I walked out of the hotel, for there was Silva standing by his bus, waiting either to say goodbye, or to have me return with him to Caracas on the bus. He had been waiting for two hours for my decision. He gave me a great big hug and said, 'Not to worry, Brian, not to worry. I know, pressures! Modern life. You find beautiful woman on top of Roraima, and bring her back to me!'

To top it all there were three Toyota landcruisers, their respective drivers and several Pemon Indian porters all smiling and nodding. They had all been waiting too! I was mortified and after a deluge of apologies, I tried to become invisible and shrank into the front seat of the nearest vehicle.

At this point, Anthony came over to me and said, quietly, 'Look, Brian, are you absolutely sure about going on. Silva is going back to Caracas now and this is your last chance to go back for the film.'

'No,' I replied, 'I'm determined to go on to Roraima.'

Anthony nodded, climbed aboard, and we were on our way.

Anthony rolled out a map (he loves maps) and showed me the route that we would be taking.

'We are taking the Gold Route, which leads to El Dorado, which is quite civilized, if somewhat rustic, and jam-packed with shops advertising

"*Compra/Vento Degro*", the buying and selling of gold. You interested in gold, Professor Challenger?'

It was good to hear him call me Challenger again, and I felt that I had rejoined the expedition.

'Not remotely. Dinosaurs – yes! Do you think I'll find one, Nick?'

'Brian,' responded the handsome Adonis from the back seat, 'I think that you are a dinosaur.'

We all laughed. It was sweet of everyone to be so kind to me.

We passed towns and villages, but my mind was focused on sky and forest.

'What are you thinking about, Challenger?' asked Anthony.

'Oh . . . I'm sending out prehistoric messages to the fearsome snakes of the Gran Sabana.'

'What are you telling them, Brian?' asked Maz.

'To avoid you like the plague, in case you hit them on the bonce with your stick.'

'We won't come across snakes, will we, Anthony?' said Maz, nervously.

'Well,' replied our gallant leader, 'sometimes you can come across the bushmaster. They can grow up to 10 feet [3 m] long and they have long fangs which can penetrate leather.'

'Oh my God!' gasped Maz.

The route south started to climb the hills leading to the Gran Sabana. We stopped for a quick coffee and Anthony walked with me to point out a tree.

'See that? It is a strangler fig tree. Monkeys climb the host tree and their droppings contain fig seeds that they deposit in fissures in the bark. These grow and become vines and live off the host tree, until they entirely cover it and strangle it to death. The tree inside becomes a dead husk. There are all kinds of rodents living in the tiny crevices and hollows. By the way, if you care to look over your shoulder, what do you see?'

In the distance I could see clouds hiding a large dark mountain.

'What is it, Anthony?' I asked him, puzzled by his question.

After a brief pause he said softly, 'That is Roraima.'

'Shouldn't the earth shake?' I whispered.

He smiled and said, 'It's over 100 miles [160 km] away.'

I boarded the landcruiser in a daze and we continued to climb the escarpment. Massive trees shaded us on either side of the road and after a few more miles of rain forest we arrived at the entrance to the Gran Sabana. There, before us, on the right-hand side of the road was a huge billboard with a painting of the Sabana and Angel Falls. It was early evening and the mists of the rain forest mingled with the pink and dark blue skies above. The evening was still, my breathing slowed, and I could hear my heart throbbing loudly.

We still had quite a way to go and it was nearly dark when we arrived at our campsite in Kamoiran. Yes, we were camping tonight, no hotel! With the help of the Pemon Indians we pitched our tents on a circle of dry clay, which was close to some small rustic houses, homes of the Pemon Indians. We were, at last, in the wilderness. Indian children sat and watched us, and they smiled and laughed almost as much as their parents.

Of course, the local children thought I was a hoot. Bearded and heavy, they thought I was some kind of ape-man. After dinner, we wished them, and each other, a good night, and what a blissful night it was. Trillions of stars pulsated, while bright fleeting meteors raced across the heavens. In my tent I was as snug as a bug in a rug, and slept like a stone.

Breakfast was quite leisurely the following morning and we all practised archery with the Pemon Indians and their children. One young lad was really terrific. Of course they used real bows and arrows, and they fairly zapped into the trees surrounding the camp. I had done a little archery with a long bow, so it was interesting to try to apply my technique to their bows. It worked quite well, but in the inevitable competition, the young ones trounced us.

We left the Pemon village and headed toward our destination. It was a remarkable journey and I kept stopping the vehicle to take more shots. At last we reached the entrance to Canaima National Park and from here the road climbed through the lush forest of the Serrania De Lema. We stopped and drank from some picturesque little waterfalls. When we emerged from the forest, the vast expanse of the great high Gran Sabana stretched out in a simply unforgettable panorama.

People say to me, 'Brian Blessed, you must grow up.' 'Never,' I reply, 'I must grow down and not lose touch with the child in me.'

There were rolling hills, covered with flowing grasses. Rivers snaked through it, bordered by moriche palms, and, in the cobalt blue distance, the first of the ancient *tepuis* could be seen. My senses reeled at the sight of this mighty landscape. We took a slight detour to see the Apanguao river and feasted our bulging eyes on the spectacular falls, known as Chinak-Meru. They are about 400 feet (120 m) across and 600 feet (182 m) high and the volume and power of the water is awesome. I sat on a boulder close to the base where the fresh spray peppered my bearded face. What wonder! What epic, majestic scenery!

I bought several blowpipes and darts from some Pemon Indians who had laid out dozens of them on the grass and rocks. They are deadly weapons and easy to master and I think we all bought enough to start a small war.

Sadly, we had to leave this staggering place, for we could hear the siren call of the Goddess Kuin from the summit of Roraima, and we longed to taste her cassava-based liquor – *Kachiri*. In other words, we needed to get a move on.

12

RORAIMA

The nearest village to Roraima is Perai Tepui, an Indian community, which has a radio station. On arrival, we unloaded our camping gear and stored it in a large shed. Explore had employed local porters to carry our food, tents and equipment, but we had to carry our personal gear. Though an additional porter could be hired for £35–£40 to carry this if you wished. The hike to Roraima is graded as 'moderate' to 'strenuous' and it was planned that we would get to the summit in three days. We would stay there for three days and then come down. We would trek for two days, for five or seven hours a day, to reach our base camp below the mountain on time.

Any group wishing to visit Roraima has to be accompanied by an Indian guide. This includes excursions that have travelled independently, and groups organized by tour operators like our own. Indian guides can be hired in San Francisco de Yuruani or Perai Tepui de Roraima. Their function is not only to lead the group but to prevent excursionists from damaging the environment. It is a fact that tourists who have climbed the *tepui* without a guide are responsible for the worst damage caused to Mount Roraima. Moreover, the groups without a guide have also suffered most of the accidents on the mountain. It is as easy as pie to break a leg on this strenuous route, and the weather is unpredictable and dangerous. On the way to Roraima there are several rivers of medium volume that swell unexpectedly to a much greater size. Only the guides know the best places to camp to avoid the risk of becoming trapped and isolated between two swollen rivers. They also know the safest places to cross and the best way to prevent a group from becoming split up.

Roraima is no picnic!

It was about 10.00 a.m. and the temperature was already almost 30°C (86°F). It was going to be a stinking hot day. The weather would normally be tropical; baking hot equatorial sun, and frequent heavy rain showers.

For the off I was dressed in a light black T-shirt and long safari trousers. I had plenty of gear in my rucksack, including two marvellous long, light, waterproof macs. I also wore a green 'Tilly' hat which is great in any weather. I greased up, put on my sunglasses and, after spraying my arms with insect repellent, moved off with the group. We had six strong and cheerful porters with us, so what with them and our leader, Anthony, we were in good hands.

After a few minutes, I was sweating like a pig, I was not as acclimatized to the heat as I thought. Ah well, only 12 miles (19 km) to go, I thought, before we camp.

My main concern was how to protect my video camera. It had performed very well so far but I had not yet subjected it to the heavy rain of Venezuela. The landscape was utterly divine and Anthony came alongside to point out various *tepuis*, ending with Roraima, which was growing larger by the minute. My thoughts and emotions were in a state of happy chaos. I tried to control my excitement, but as my hero, George Leigh Mallory once said of Everest, 'Lord, when I think of it, something bubbles up inside me. The effervescence is sternly repressed, of course, and then a bubble outs and bursts!'

Anthony was gratified by my enthusiasm, for he adored Venezuela.

Nick was in the lead, with Maz close to his shoulder and Janet and Karen not far behind with their husbands keeping a wary eye on them. Sometimes I would rush ahead to get a tracking shot of the group. We were moving along nicely and shortly we reached our first obstacle.

We had to cross a wide, boulder-strewn river, which was called the Rio Maturu Paru. Two of the porters got across and tied a strong rope to one of the boulders whilst Anthony secured it on our side. I wanted to film everybody crossing, so, not trusting myself with the camera, I gave it to one of the porters called Babeto who had by now become 'my personal guide and camera assistant'.

The river surprised me. I thought that it would be a piece of cake. Not so. The current was deceptively strong and I had a lot of difficulty keeping my balance. I kept my boots on as the river bed was stony but later that proved to be a mistake. The others came over in a long line and they were also surprised by the strength of the current. Safely across we continued on our way.

The huge expanse of the high savanna went on and on and on. It was raining one minute, sunshine the next. Here and there were dotted clumps of rain forest. Alongside Roraima was the other great *tepui* Mount Kukenan (the Sacred Mountain). The correct name of this *tepui,* which is only 426 feet (130 m) lower than Roraimai is Matawi-Tepui. 'Matawi' means 'I want to die' or 'a place to commit suicide'.

When Pemon warriors were defeated by Makushi invaders from the territory which is called Brazil today, or when they were rejected in love, the overwhelmed Indians jumped to their death from this *tepui.* Their bodies were destroyed by a mythological being called 'Matawi'. However, the *tepui* has become known as Kukenan because the river of that name originates on its summit. The Kukenan waterfall has an uninterrupted drop of 2,000 feet (610 m), and is the second highest freefall cascade in Venezuela. Though it was a good 30 miles (48 kms) away it looked gigantic and forbidding.

'A very sinister place,' said Anthony. 'I've been to its summit and I found it very depressing.'

As we moved on, I thought how incredible it was that we were walking on earth that was two billion years old. We were following in the footsteps of Everard im Thurn.

We stopped for lunch in a forest glade beside a gently flowing stream. I decided to explore the forest a little and to film some of the plants. I found several small pools and waterfalls of sheer delight. The draped thickets and tangled undergrowth contained numerous tiny orchids. Hummingbirds, darts of brilliant green and blue, visited one flower after another. The soft vibrations of their wings charmed the senses and they didn't seem to be bothered by my presence. I could see dozens of pink and white flowers, some were faded and dying, while others looked robust and young.

I had been motionless for about a minute, when I jumped out of my skin! A blue morpho butterfly whizzed past me. I was convinced that it was a *Morpho rhetenor*, one of the eighty species of the family of Morphidae. The *rhetenor* is probably my favourite. It is azure blue, with two delicate white spots near the tip of its wings. Relative to its body size, its wing span is large and this gives it an effortless flight action. It made my heart miss a beat. I had wanted to see one in the wild and I raced back to the lunching party and gasping with excitement, 'I've seen a blue morpho!'

Anthony smiled and nodded for the umpteenth time.

'Such enthusiasm, Challenger, is lovely to behold but come and have some lunch.'

So I did, and afterwards we set off again.

I was feeling great, I stepped out on the red, rusty path and we rapidly gained height and distance. After about 6 miles (10 km) I stopped on a bright green hillock to examine my feet. I had two bloody awful big blisters. After all the expeditions I had been on, I was disgusted with myself that I'd allowed this to happen. I should not have kept my boots on at the river crossing, they had become slack and had rubbed both my heel and instep. I applied cream and plasters, but the damage was done. I would have to walk through the pain, because nothing was going to stop me going to Roraima.

Two miles (3.2 km) further on we reached our camp. It was a good site with the river Tek Paru running nearby so we could bathe and fill our water bottles. It was then that I noticed that my arms had been badly bitten. Blood was dripping off them and I hadn't felt a thing. Some of the others had suffered the same fate.

'You have got to use stronger sprays. The midges just laugh at what you have been using,' advised Anthony.

He then gave us all a bottle from his rucksack and said, 'You may stand a fighting chance with that.'

Shortly afterward, we congregated in the dining area which was a large tin hut with a chair or two and some rustic benches. Anthony and Babeto prepared another scrumptious meal, whilst we, brown and glowing, chattered and laughed and relaxed. We were so relieved, at last, to be travelling under our own steam.

The lamps attracted all manner of creepy crawlies. The floor of the hut was covered in sand and several of the group were bare footed.

'You know,' said Anthony, 'you have got to be aware of the "jiggers".'

'What're "jiggers"?' said Maz, swiping a strange insect from her shoulder.

'Well, jiggers live in sand, particularly in this area, and burrow into your feet where they lay their eggs. They are very hard to remove as they burrow deep and you would normally need a doctor to dig them out, although usually I can remove them. Sometimes you even need to have an operation. They are short, black things, like leeches. The eggs don't hatch for weeks but when they do they burrow through your feet.'

At this point, of course, Maz said, 'Oh, my God!' and as she said it an insect about 4 inches (10 cm) long landed on her face. Naturally, Maz let out a huge shriek at the unannounced visitor. There was pandemonium, and I have never laughed so much in my life.

For the rest of the evening Anthony told lurid stories about rare diseases, and snakes that attack without provocation. As we finished our coffee he ended the evening by telling us about the 'twenty-four-hour ant'.

'Twenty-four-hour ant, what's that?' Maz said.

'Well,' said Anthony, 'It doesn't kill you unless you have got a weak heart, but it's a big ant, about an inch long, and it's got a very painful bite, and for twenty-four hours you are in agony.'

Maz's face said it all. 'Oh, my God!'

We all retired to our tents and made a thorough inspection of all our belongings before we could go to sleep.

The next day we crossed the shallow, slow-flowing, Maturu Paru river and started to gain more height as we headed for base camp. There were several other expeditions on the mountain. Some were suffering badly from the heat and giving up and going down but others were strong and organized like us. The heat was terrible and we panted like old English sheepdogs. It was about another 8 miles (13 km) to base camp and I was reminded of a few lines from *The Lost World*,

> *We were within seven miles of an enormous line of ruddy red cliffs which encircled, beyond all doubt, the plateau of which Professor Challenger spoke.*

As we paused for breath I told Karen that way back down the valley, beyond Perai Tepui, you come to San Francisco de Yuruani, from where it is possible to see the west side of Roraima, which is known as the Golden Wall. At the south end there is a huge section that seems to be separated from Roraima. It is called Tevasin, which means 'stone to put the pot on the fire'. In the novel, Professor Challenger and his companions climbed the mountain through this sector – and not a lot of people know that!

Karen laughed, and thanked me and we joined forces up a steep hill, encouraging each other every step of the way. Then the heavens opened and before we had time to put on our waterproofs, we were drenched to the skin. Great black nimbus clouds enveloped Roraima until it almost disappeared from sight. Numerous waterfalls poured over the edge of the cliff. Then, just as suddenly, the sun came out, and the deep red colour on parts of the vertical precipices stood out from the sombre forest below.

. . . delicious paradise,
Now nearer, crowns with her enclosure green,
As with a rural mound the champaign head
Of steep wilderness, whose hairy sides
With thicket overgrown, grotesque and wild,
Access denied; and over head up grew
Insuperable height of loftiest shade
Cedar, and pine, and fir, and branching palm,
A sylvan scene, and as the ranks ascend
Shade above shade, a woody theatre,
Of stateliest view.'

John Milton, *Paradise Lost*, Book IV

The storm had ceased and a strange silence replaced the turmoil. My heart pounded, and my mind became still as the silence deepened. The towering cliffs were stunning and intimidating. Such stillness and harmony. Sporadic white clouds hovered motionless against the soft pinks and beige of the rugged walls. Janet and Miles joined Karen and myself and I said simply, 'I've wanted to see this since I was a child.'

Someone had to break the spell and it was Babeto,

'Your camera – you will film – yes?'

'Yes,' I smiled, and I did.

Half an hour later we were at base camp and set up our tents. Everyone was tense and quiet at dinner but we smiled and wished each other good fortune. Roraima looked haunting and blood-red in the fading light.

Then the whole ambience of the evening was shattered by the sudden appearance, and sound, of a large helicopter. It was a Brazilian film crew, bursting with energy, who were filming Roraima. The helicopter moved high up the ramparts of the great mountain and then plunged aggressively towards us, before pulling to the right to take shots of distant Kukenan.

The helicopter made one more pass and finally disappeared out of sight. The whole process reminded me of a passage in *The Lost World*:

Suddenly out of the darkness, out of the night, there swooped something
with a swish like an airplane. The whole group of us were covered for
an instant by a canopy of leathery wings, and I had momentary vision

of a long, snakelike neck, a fierce, red, greedy eye and a great snapping beak, filled, to my amazement, with little, gleaming teeth. The next instant it was gone – and so was our dinner. A huge black shadow, twenty feet across, skimmed up into the air; for an instant the monster with wings blotted out the stars, and then it vanished over the brow of the cliff above us.

It is interesting to note later in the book how Howard Malone describes the pterodactyls in their pit,

At first the great brutes flew round in a huge ring. Then the flight grew louder and the circle narrower, until they were whizzing round us, the dry, rustling flap of their huge slate coloured wings filling the air with a volume of sound that made me think of Hendon Aerodrome upon a race day.

Had he been with us, Sir Arthur Conan Doyle might perhaps have approved of the visitation from the helicopter. After all he had enjoyed his own first aeroplane flight at Hendon in 1911. But would he have approved of ladies being on our expedition? In his book, the intrepid explorers are all men.

My eyes now turned from the great silent wall of Roraima to my companions. They all stood still as statues. The moment was sacred. Tim and Karen gently embraced, Maz joined hands with Nick, and Miles and Janet just stared transfixed as the two lads, David and Andrew, scratched their heads and gazed in wonder. This is what they had come for. To see and climb the Lost World. The mighty cliffs of Roraima turned to blackness, as the sun sank from sight. Tomorrow was going to be a big day.

It was madly exciting to think that we would actually be ascending the mountain by the same route as Everard im Thurn and Harry I Perkins, in 1884. They were the very first men to climb it. Everard im Thurn wrote an account in the journal of the Royal Agricultural and Commercial Society of British Guyana, in June 1885,

We found that the path (to the foot of the ledge) had been cleared only just sufficiently to allow us to pass, and that not without considerable difficulty.

'Seldom if ever did we step on the real ground, but instead we climbed, hands and feet all fully employed, over masses of vegetation dense enough to bear our weight, over high-piled rocks and tree trunks and along tree branches, across the beds of many streams so filled with broken rocks that the water heard trickling below was unseen. Nor did the dense and universal coating of moss, filmy ferns and lung-worts afford any but the most treacherous foothold and handhold.

The way, which was very difficult and wearisome though at no point dangerous, was again over, under and along more tree roots, branches and trunks, again over and up steep slopes of wet slippery mud – tree, rock and mud being alike wrapped in the usual covering of wet moss. Over such ground as this we made our way round the three spurs, and at last came in sight of the part of the ledge on to which falls the stream from above. A fairly gentle slope, covered with coarse grass, taller than ourselves, led down, for a considerable distance, to the actual point on to which the water fell, which, to our great delight, we saw was no deep impassable pool or ravine, but a broad, sloping reach of broken rocks; on the other side of this, the ledge sloped almost as gradually upward, but this upward slope consisted for some distance of a slippery expanse of rock, broken by faintly marked step-like ledges, over the whole of which in the heavy rainy season a continuous flood of water must pour, but which was now almost dry. At last the way to the top lay before us clear, and, if somewhat difficult, certainly passable.

Up this part of the slope we made our way with comparative ease. Then the step was taken – and we saw surely as strange a sight, regarded simply as a product of nature, as may be seen in this world; nay it would probably not be too rash to assert that very few sights even as strange can be seen. The first impression was one of inability mentally to grasp such surroundings; the next that one was entering on some strange country of nightmares for which an appropriate and wildly fantastic landscape had been formed, some dreadful and stormy day, when, in their mid-career, the broken and chaotic clouds stiffened, in a single instant, into stone. For all around were rocks and pinnacles of rocks of seemingly impossibly fantastic forms, standing in apparently fantastic ways – nay placed one on, or next to, the other in positions seeming to defy gravity – rocks in groups, rocks standing singly, rocks *in terraces, rocks as columns, rocks as walls and rocks as pyramids, rocks ridiculous at every point with countless apparent caricatures of the faces and forms of men and animals, apparent caricatures of umbrellas, tortoises, churches, cannons, and of innumerable other most incongruous and unexpected objects. And, between the rocks were level spaces, never of great extent, of pure yellow sand, with streamlets of little waterfalls and pools and shallow lakelets of pure water; and in some places there were little marshes filled with low scanty and bristling vegetation. And here and there, alike on level space and jutting from some crevice in the rock, were small shrubs in form like miniature trees, but all apparently of one species. Not a tree was there, no animal life was visible or, it even seemed, so intensely quiet and undisturbed did the place look, ever had been there. Look where one would on every side it was the same; and climb what high rock one liked, in every direction, as far as the eye could see was this same wildly extraordinary scenery.*

'Notes by Alexander Laime in 1955'

How do I follow that, dear readers? Well, I did follow that, or rather, him. We all followed him at precisely 7.00 a.m. on 10 July 1998.

It was raining like hell and the steep slopes leading to the dense rain forest were awash with mud, muck, and twisted branches. But did we care? No! We were alive and well and our veins were pounding with adrenalin. My feet were in a right bloody mess. Anthony had patched them up but you could see my bones through the burst blisters.

It is the sense of heightened awareness and perception of beauty, of being alive, of physical accomplishment, that raises adventure despite periods of mind-blowing agony, from being an exercise in masochism to a much broader, richer experience.

Sir Christian Bonington, *Quest for Adventure*

The mud was really bad and to assist our balance we just grabbed hard tree roots and anything else that came to hand. It was not quite the weather that we had hoped for and I didn't help myself by trying to continue filming. Still, I had my faithful Babeto at my side, so how could I fail? But the camera was now taking quite a beating. We continued to move up, climbing higher and higher and crossed overgrown ledges to the base of the wall. The rain forest here is jam-packed with bromeliads, ferns, pitcher plants, orchids and trumpet flowers. The vegetation was vigorously green. A thick carpet of moss and liverworts covered the ground and the track was overgrown with bushes. I would take twenty steps forward, and then fall flat on my face. It was quite impossible to maintain any kind of rhythm, but I was enjoying myself and forgot the pain in my feet. The filming slowed me down and so I was falling way behind the others. You simply could not hurry in all that slime and rain or you'd break a leg.

We were all gripped by 'Tepui Fever'. The track steepened and as I rounded a rocky area I walked straight into a cascading waterfall and got completely soaked. It was noticeably colder and both Babeto and I were covered in mud and wet leaves. At times I felt as though I was imprisoned by plants. Then much to my relief we reached the base of the cliff. Bromeliads, with their trough-like rosettes of leaves, clung to trees and cliffs. I came across an astonishing emerald green moss wall. Anthony told me later that it is one of the great features of Roraima. There I was covered in muck and leaves and my blisters were singing the 'Hallelujah Chorus', and yet I was dizzy with joy. Every foot I gained increased my excitement. I looked up the sheer wall of Roraima and it was half covered in mysterious mist. Was there no end to these wonders? The end, in fact, was coming dramatically, for I had reached about 9,000 feet (2,743 m), only a little way to go.

Babeto and I started to laugh, as we stood under a wide delicate waterfall and hugged each other. He was nonplussed as I quoted Wilhelm Bittorf with glee:

> *To find adventure on a tame planet, the children of comfort plunge themselves into ever more bizarre escapades.*
> Rene Ferlet and Guy Poulet, *Aconcagua South Face*

Babeto and I were living proof of that. We moved away from the waterfall and shook ourselves like a pair of water spaniels. Then we moved upwards on to firmer ground towards a break in the cliff and I saw Anthony ahead waving us up.

I shook with happiness, savouring every moment, as I moved towards him. My mind conjured up Mr Brown, the headmaster, who caned me when I was a small boy for listening to *The Lost World* on the radio. I remembered all my school chums who kept me company by my favourite stream the Gam, and whom I had urged in my boyish enthusiasm to go to the Lost World. I placed my feet on top of a boulder and my mind returned to the present and Anthony's gentle voice whispered, 'Welcome to the Lost World'. I shook hands with every member of our splendid team.

EPILOGUE

The word 'epilogue' always brings a smile to my face. It reminds me of that American science fiction TV series, *The Invaders*. You remember it? The titles would start with throbbing, atmospheric music, followed by a deep voice saying 'The Invaders'! The last five minutes of each episode was devoted to the 'Epilogue', followed by the end credits and the same deep voice saying, 'This is a Quinn Martin Production'. Well this 'Epilogue' is a 'Brian Blessed Production'. I felt it appropriate to write one, as you might feel that my tale of the Lost World ended rather abruptly. I felt it right to end it there, because my childhood dream had been fulfilled. But I also feel that I need to tie up a few loose ends.

On the 9,094-foot (2,771 m) summit of that enormous, primeval, sandstone mesa we saw hundreds of astonishing rocks with shapes and profiles that resembled gargoyles, Indian deities, Egyptian statues and Cambodian temples. Some of these ancient rocks have colourful names, such as Fierce Wolf, the Monkey Eating Ice Cream, the Flying Turtle and the Ford Maverick.

We managed to penetrate a few yards into the unexplored Great Labyrinth of the North. One day I intend to return to the Labyrinth with Steve Bell, Anthony, and Ramon Blanco. Using ropes, two-way radios, and frogmen's outfits, we might be able to penetrate deeper and unlock some of its secrets. Who knows what we may discover? It is rumoured that there are vast caverns of diamonds to be found in the Labyrinth. The Pemon Indians would not set foot in it for love nor money. They gave no reason for this, they just shook their heads. Perhaps they fear they will be haunted by Corupuri, the Spirit of the Woods, or incur the displeasure of the Goddess Kuin. Like Theseus, when we explore it, we might encounter a

South American Minotaur. I wonder what sort of creature makes those terrible screams that are frequently heard in that sinister place.

When we ascended the plateau, we came across nothing faintly resembling a Tyrannosaurus rex or pterodactyl, but we did meet a tiny little black toad, with black spots on a yellow belly, called *Oreophrynella quelchii*. He was a lovely little fella. This species, discovered on Roraima in 1894, retains primitive traits, not because of isolation, but because the environment has not forced it to change. Barely an inch (2.5 cm) long, it cannot hop or swim. We were surprised to discover that Roraima has the world's only underwater crickets. Press your ears just under the surface of a pool and you can hear a chirrup. Also, much to my astonishment, I filmed a large coatimundi up there. How did it manage to get up? Beats me!

For three days we experienced a deluge that Noah himself would have found intimidating. Roraima is truly 'The Mother of All Waters'. Torrential rain created mighty waterfalls that poured down its great precipices, to bring life to the valleys below. We stood near the edge of those fantastic cliffs and saw the waterfalls tumbling down and disappearing out of sight into dense mist, created by the impact of water hitting the ground below. We had to be careful as it was quite windy. A year earlier, a German woman taking a photograph had got too near to the edge and had been blown over to her death.

I looked over my right shoulder. About a mile away was the Diamond Waterfall, plunging down into the Paikna Watershed. Close by is a canyon, so magical, that it seems to have been drawn from a fairy tale by Hans Christian Anderson. The ground consists entirely of sparkling pink and white crystals. This is the Valley of the Crystals named by Doctor Brewer-Carias, who discovered the canyon in 1976. We swam there in a cool, small lake of shining delight. The canyon ends abruptly on the east side of Roraima, where a waterfall pours over an outcrop of crystal. The light reflects from it with such intensity that Roraima becomes the vibrant watch tower of the Gran Sabana. The legend of Sir Walter Raleigh's Crystal Mountain is made real.

There are times on Roraima when the power of the water underground feels almost seismic. It is as if some vast subterranean powerhouse is pumping water through great rivers of darkness. Take the Great Labyrinth itself. It is a 3-square-mile (7.7 sq km) region of jumbled rock towers and awesome chasms. In successive ages of erosion the water has cut fantastic channels within channels in the depths of these forbidding chasms. There are different levels of chamber that in the rainy season fill with raging water with great rapidity. A few months before we arrived a group of men had attempted to explore it, and all but one had disappeared. The survivor was found unconscious and bleeding from head to foot by Taurepan Indians. Shuddering with pain and horror he described how the expedition had advanced about 150 feet (46 m), when it started to rain. Within minutes they were exposed to the full power of the wind and a blinding massive force of water. The empty, dry channels filled with rampaging, cold water forming rivers that foamed and tossed them about like corks. The men were torn to pieces. The sole survivor was lucky to be alive. Such is the power of the Mother of All Waters.

Nevertheless, Roraima, for me, is the eighth wonder of the world. Bromeliads endure both intense solar radiation and cool, humid conditions. Deprived of nutrients from soil, they catch their own, digesting insects that fall into the water in their throats. Bromeliads are a wide-ranging tropical family, but only on *tepuis* have they displayed this carnivorous behaviour. Soil on the summit is scarce. The floor is mainly rock and no footprints are left on it. Hence, there are almost no paths. The topographical irregularities that I have mentioned make it impossible to advance in a straight line or to remember the way back on Roraima.

People are often surprised to hear there are hotels on the summit. However these 'so-called' hotels are actually just caves in the rocks which serve as a refuge from unexpected showers and cold night-time temperatures, which can fall as low as 0°C (32°F). Only guides know their exact location and the routes to them. They are the only ones who know the maximum number of places that can be visited each day, as well as when it is time to go back to the refuges before mist and darkness make it difficult or impossible to return to a safe place. We stayed in what is called 'The Grand Hotel', a series of large caves in which we pitched our tents.

Yes, the plateau of Roraima was a fascinating landscape, but my feelings on reaching it were mixed. I am almost loathe to write about it, as it was such a splendid expedition, but in truth I felt a distressing sense of anticlimax and unhappiness. As far as I can remember, none of the other members of the expedition shared my feelings. They were wonderfully cheerful, and of course, so was I. I wasn't about to let the side down, that would hardly be fair. So I laughed and joked with the best of them. That is, until I zipped up my tent and slipped into the warm security of my sleeping bag, then I became a different creature.

I was surprised and perplexed by my emotions, my enthusiasm for reaching the Lost World had been so strong that I had allowed it to push certain impressions to the back of my mind. Now my unconscious mind asserted itself, and insisted on being heard. I suppose the rot set in when Anthony pointed out the Lost World to me from the modern road leading to the Gran Sabana. The road was on a par with the A30, near my home in Surrey. This road passes quite close to the Lost World and this reality staggered me.

We had driven on a well-constructed, wide unmade road to Perai Tepui, but what really set me back on my heels was that there was a well-worn path all the way to the base of Roraima. 'God protect me from expectation', I have always said and the words were never more relevant.

I reacted like a little boy who was disappointed by his first toffee apple. All that bottled up expectation from my childhood finally manifested itself, it was ridiculous. It never entered my head that the terrain would be any different from that experienced by Everard im Thurn in 1884; in those days Perai Tepui was covered in dense rain forest but that was over 100 years ago and of course, time marches on. Though in all fairness, I have to say, that once im Thurn had penetrated the forest, he encountered the glorious savanna which has not changed a great deal to this day, and there is no denying that from a distance, Roraima and Kukenan and the other *tepuis* are, without doubt, one of the greatest spectacles on God's Earth.

So what the hell am I carping on about? In the final analysis, it was the plateau of Roraima that bugged me. I felt as if I had no right to be there. As if I was an alien, trespassing on a forbidden world.

Tread softly, for this is Holy ground
It may be, could we look with seeing eyes
This spot we stand on is Paradise.

Christina Rossetti

The landscape on Roraima looks as though it has been constructed by Cyclops, the one-eyed giants of Greek mythology. Yet, in spite of the grandeur of its rock formations, most of the life there is in miniature. Our little friends the black toads are a perfect example. Though they are blind, they must have been alarmed by our presence as our gigantic feet sent jarring vibrations through the rocks where they lived. Everything there clings so precariously to life.

As I have mentioned, most of the mineral nutrients that are essential to plant growth have been washed away by the incessant rainfall. Miraculously, in spite of this, numerous beautiful, miniature oases bloom everywhere. I felt like a giant in this landscape. A Gulliver in a South American Lilliput. I fantasized about it as I plodded round the plateau. There in my mind's eye I saw millions of tiny Roraima Lilliputians, scattering in all directions to avoid my size eleven boots. I was painfully aware of the ancient plants around me, and I steadfastly avoided damaging them.

But it was the rocks themselves that disturbed me most of all. I am normally a good sleeper but in the two nights spent on Roraima, I doubt that I managed to get more than three hours sleep. I felt that I was living in two worlds, each as real as the other.

Though I have often been accused of having an over-active imagination, I have never been susceptible to things that go bump in the night. I had often heard about people having nightmares, but it was a condition that I had never experienced. That is, until my first night on Roraima. Then I was subjected to images that made Dante's *Inferno* look like *The Magic Roundabout*. It followed the same pattern each night. After about twenty minutes of fitful sleep, my eyes would open and I would find myself entombed in dense rock. As this happened I found myself whispering, 'The gnashing of teeth, the unmanifested universe.' Strangely enough I accepted this appalling experience and, by resisting conflict I felt a pure feeling of sacrifice. In this state, all things seemed possible. The crude rocks changed and I became an unborn child, surrounded by crystals. These dissolved and I accelerated along a vast, bright tunnel that led to a white universe with black stars. Within this weird universe I saw the most unimaginably grotesque faces. They came in all shapes and sizes, with frightful excretions pouring from their mouths and eyes. This went on for hours and towards dawn they finally faded away amidst a chorus of mumbling and moaning. Throughout the experience, I felt positive. Come what may, I thought that I would survive. It was a tangible feeling that I had always existed. Towards the end of this vision, I returned once more to be entombed in the crude rock. The pressure on my body was oppressive. The sacrificial feeling once more pervaded my whole being and finally caused the rock to split into thousands of pieces and disappear into space. I then felt released and free.

The experience occurred for two nights. I can't say that I welcomed it, as the negative part was truly horrendous and caused me to sweat profusely. On the second night there was a slight deviation when I experienced the sight and sound of vast waterfalls that transformed into billions of coloured, glass marbles. I attributed this to my childhood, as when I was 10 years old I had my ears syringed and afterwards I remember that the water from the tap sounded like marbles.

I spent one morning exploring a little on my own. Oh yes! There is no doubt at all that Sir Arthur Conan Doyle's dinosaurs are certainly on the roof of Roraima, but they are cast in stone, awaiting the magical touch of some cosmic wizard to activate them into life. Everard im Thurn was right, it is a strange landscape of fantastic nightmares. It felt as if it had not been disturbed since time began. The rock is at least 1.8 billion years old. Such vast expanses of time are incomprehensible. Roraima's sedimentary rock was already age-old when South America and Africa were joined together in the prehistoric continent now called Gondwana. Cliffs and mesa-like mountains in the western Sahara consist of sandstone similar to that on Mount Roraima.

'Lighten up, Brian,' I said to myself, 'Come on, snap out of it. Your thoughts are too heavy.'

I smiled and stroked the rocks.

'Hello Gondwana! What secrets do you hide in your ancient rocks? It is you I know who influences the reptilian part of my brain and fills my night with strange visions.'

It is widely accepted in scientific circles that in areas where tectonic plates rub up against one another, fantastic pressure is put on the crystals in the rock and they, in turn, produce electromagnetic fields. All I know is that Roraima positively hums with primeval power. For me, the solar flood of light on that ancient terrain makes the rocks and stones sing, and some of their songs can be very gloomy. These rocks are not inanimate. They are not lifeless. They are not solid. Our friends the scientists frequently describe rocks as being rather like a packet of peas: millions and millions of atoms. I am quite convinced that the mystical dance of the electrons in rocks played havoc with my receptive neo-cortex.

I moved to the point where the German woman had disappeared a year earlier. Mists came down unexpectedly and shrouded distant Kukenan. Over a period of twenty minutes or so, they cleared and that great *tepui* glistened in the morning light. Its great 2,000-feet (610 m) waterfall cascaded down uninterrupted into the forest below. How sad, I thought, that it is called 'A Place to Die'. It looked so beautiful.

As I turned and looked out towards the Gran Sabana, I imagined the Earth before organic life had come. A bizarre violent land below a poisonous sky. Yet, out of that fearful chaos came all that blooms in plants and moves in creatures. I thought of the great carboniferous forest that dominated the Earth some 350 million years ago. They stretched from horizon to horizon. They fed upon an atmosphere saturated with carbonic acid gas many times thicker than it is today. There were no birds in those trees. Just think of it, songless glades. Yet these mighty forests cleansed our atmosphere. Purification was the primary work of these trees, and there I was, a 62-year-old Yorkshire lad, standing on a great *tepui* that had been born over one billion years before those forests had emerged. What a rare privilege it was to be there. Yet I couldn't wait to leave the place. I certainly didn't want to spend another night there.

> *By the apostle Paul, shadows tonight*
> *Have struck more terror to the soul of Richard*
> *Than can the substance of ten thousand soldiers*
> *Armed in proof and led by shallow Richmond.*
>   William Shakespeare, *Richard III*, Act V, Scene iii

Possibly I was not ready for the Roraima experience. At any rate, I was mightily relieved when Anthony slapped me on the back and announced it was time to go.

An hour later we descended, or rather slipped and crawled, down the steep slopes of the mountain. After two days we arrived back to the stifling heat of Perai Tepui. From there we were driven to our rustic accommodation at Santa Elena De Varien, where we boarded a small charter plane to continue southwards across the Gran Sabana, with extraordinary panoramas on all sides. Oh Venezuela! Venezuela! A territory of superlatives. It has a mystic quality. The forest was a gigantic mosaic in different shades of green. Here, there and everywhere, were our old friends the *tepuis*. Rows and rows and rows of them as far as the eye could see. On and on we flew and landed at the missionary settlement of Kamarata. Here we slept in hammocks and drove on the next day, through rough terrain to the Indian village of Kavak. There, rising above the rain forest was our next destination, Mount Auyan Tepui. This is the largest *tepui* in the Gran Sabana, with 270 square miles (700 sq km) of jungle, deserts, rivers and rocky terrain. So little of it is known. Here Alexander Laime claimed he encountered dinosaur-like lizards that resembled plesiosaurs, marine reptiles that became extinct 65 million years ago. The name

'Auyan Tepui' means 'Hell's Mountain'. Kamaracoto Indian mythology says that at top of the mountain live 'Hawaritan' – the evil spirits – and that it is the Kingdom of Traman-Chita, the God of Evil.

From the Indian village we scrambled over boulders and plunged into a fast-moving stream and headed for a deep narrow inlet. We swam up this inlet and penetrated into the bowels of Devil's Canyon. We could hear a roar ahead of us, and on we went, fighting the current, and taking deep breaths whenever we could. Then suddenly we arrived in a huge cavern the size of a cathedral. There was a great hole in the side of the roof from which poured a great waterfall. It produced a roar that reverberated around the sheer walls of the cavern. On every side water poured and rushed into the warm, deep pool. Some of the rock was covered in a spongy fibrous mass of moss, and when I pressed it, a rich red pigment ran out. 'Red Bacteria', shouted one of the Kamaracoto Indians.

The pure water and the energy of the waterfall was so wonderful that it felt as if it was penetrating every nook and cranny of my brain, and washing away the ghastly images I had experienced on Roraima. We couldn't stop laughing and shouting with happiness. We swam underwater and made ridiculous faces at one another like Charles Kingsley's Water Babies. We swam back down the inlet like a set of demented river otters and entered a tiny valley full of crystal clear ponds and numerous waterfalls. It felt like the third day of Genesis. Water, water, everywhere and lots and lots to drink! Our excitement was unquenchable. You could run fifty times around the moon, and it still wouldn't have been as wonderful as this.

Isn't it ridiculous? In our so-called 'civilized world', that we cannot actually drink a pure cup of water. We stand on the Earth and look up. Water falls from the heavens – and we cannot have it. Plants and animals can drink it, but not humans. That is the situation today. We dare not risk drinking from our rivers unless the water has been treated. Instead, we raise our hands in gratitude to the water companies for supplying us with liquid that will not poison us. I certainly have never had any desire to drink chlorinated water. The water that we were drinking at the base of Auyan Tepui was full of minerals and invisible organic life. When this protozaic life is magnified, it looks like daisies, starfish, birds, elephants and ice crystals. As I drank it I could feel my taste buds being revitalized and every vein in my body tingled with health.

'God, this is good,' I shouted.

'Certainly is, Challenger,' Anthony responded. 'Would you mind filming me diving off that waterfall?' he shyly enquired.

'Of course not, Anthony. Go for it.'

His actions sparked off a whole series of activities from the rest of the gang. We frolicked for about half an hour, until our energy started to subside. The euphoria gradually evaporated and we were left feeling strangely listless. This was unexpected and it fascinated me. Even the heroic Nick Moss declined to jump from a rock into a deep pool below, something he would ordinarily have adored.

We walked sombrely back to the Indian village of Kavak. Mighty Auyan Tepui stretched out as far as the eye could see. Between it and the village were numerous high hills covered in dense rain and cloud forests. It was now late in the afternoon and the tropical sun was setting rapidly. Everyone moved lethargically as I filmed them feeding a couple of red and blue macaws. We had an hour to wait until the truck could take us the 15 miles (24 km) back to Kamarata. For a brief moment I entertained the thought of teasing Maz about 'jiggers' and snakes, and then I felt better of it and dismissed the idea. After a short space of time the light started to fade and it became quite gloomy. Clouds were gathering and it was about to rain. Auyan Tepui looked dark and forbidding in the background and there was something sinister and threatening about it. The sky though, was astonishing. I have never seen such colours. It was covered in dark purple and green altocumulus cloud. Now and then the dying rays of the sun would flicker on the edges of these clouds in a desperate attempt to make them look natural. It all looked surreal and the silence was deafening.

The lorry arrived and all the young uns got in the back, whilst I sat in the front with the driver. After we had travelled for a minute or two I asked him to stop. I just couldn't resist filming the sky as its colours had intensified. I was determined to make a good job of it, and so I assembled my tripod, which took quite a while. Meanwhile, everyone in the back of the truck was getting restless, and it was beginning to spit with rain.

'Come on, Brian,' they shouted. 'It's going to rain and we'll all get soaked.'

It goes without saying that I am not the best technician in the world and I was having difficulty screwing the camera on to the tripod. Their protestations were understandable as they were sitting in the back, unprotected from the expected rain, whereas I would have the luxury of a roof over my head. To cut a long story short, I lost my rag.

'For God's sake, just bugger off and leave me. I'll walk back to bloody Kamarata. It's not that far and then none of you will get bloody wet! For Christ's sake, the poxy bloody rain is warm anyway. No bugger is going to get pneumonia.'

There was a long silence which was eventually broken by Nick, who gallantly tried to placate me. The ladies were stunned, in fact we were all stunned and I couldn't believe that I had said it. What in God's name is the matter with me? I thought. Anyway I couldn't face going back with them after that tirade and I passionately urged them to go. They did so, reluctantly.

I watched the truck disappear down the narrow road through the rain forest. I was now too upset to film, so I packed everything in my rucksack and began the long walk back to Kamarata. After a while I turned and looked back at Auyan Tepui. I was convinced it had affected my behaviour. Oh, I know that I am no saint, and that I can be a prickly pear on occasions but this was something different. 'Hell's Mountain' is what they call it, and it is aptly named. I wasn't imagining this, that sinister *tepui* had cast its spell on the expedition for hours, only the smiling face of Anthony seemed free of it.

I was on my own and the darkness was almost on me. Here and there a flicker of blue lightning lit the strange sky but it failed to rain. It was unnervingly still and there wasn't a breath of wind. I began to admonish myself, 'You silly old bastard,' I said. 'Serves you right having to walk, you stupid pillock. How could you be such a pig to those lovely young people?'

It's funny how you talk to yourself in the wilderness. Even though I was ashamed of myself I still found Brian Blessed's company acceptable. My eyes became accustomed to the dark and I could see the rough path clearly, and I began to find the experience of being alone in the rain forest strangely enjoyable. After all, this is something that I had longed for since I was a child. Of course, I had experienced being alone in the Himalayas, but this was entirely different. In front of me was a never-ending carpet of black trees, broken only by dark glades. A cacophony of sound rose up from the jungle. I made steady progress along the path as the cloak of night enveloped me.

As I rounded a corner I came face to face with two Kamaracoto Indians, who were naked except for their loincloths. They both carried spears and a rustic lamp which they lifted up to peer into my face. It was a meeting of two worlds. They drew back a pace and gasped in shock. It was obvious that they had never before seen a Westerner in these surroundings and at that time of night. I was wearing a long dark waterproof with the hood over my head so I must have looked like a creature from another planet or possibly they thought I was the evil one himself, 'Traman-Chita'. Anyway, they retreated as fast as their legs could carry them.

'It's all right,' I shouted. But my voice seemed to panic them even more and they almost collided with one another in a desperate effort to escape.

A few minutes later, two orange eyes appeared in the darkness. No, they didn't belong to the Cobra Grande but to the truck, which had returned to pick me up.

'Professor Challenger, I presume,' said Anthony, smiling.

'Yes,' I replied, 'and I assume that you are Lord John Roxton.'

'Yes, indeed,' he nodded, 'please get into the truck, you've frightened everyone, I'm afraid.'

As I sat in the truck alongside him, he produced a fat bottle of brandy, and we toasted each other's health. On the journey back I expressed my regrets at what had happened and apologised a thousand times. When we arrived in Kamarata, I entered the rustic dining room where my dear friends were about to start dinner. I needn't have been apprehensive for they all looked at me with huge grins on their faces. I stared at them for a couple of seconds and then said,

'Please can you forgive a silly old tit for being such a drama queen?'

Their warm response was as big as the Orinoco and I was subjected to hugs and kisses that were totally undeserved.

'What's for dinner?' I said.

'Lots of gorgeous soup to start with, Brian,' Nick responded.

'And lots of meat and potatoes to follow,' laughed Janet.

'And, of course, Challenger, we wouldn't think of depriving you of your large milky, sweet mug of coffee at the end of the evening,' said Anthony.

'Thank God you came back to pick me up, Anthony,' I said. 'My blisters were giving me hell.' There was much laughter!

'Oh, by the way,' I continued, 'I hear that somebody on the expedition next door has been riddled with "jiggers".'

'Oh, my God,' gasped Maz.

God, I thought, I'm a lucky fella to be with such a grand bunch of youngsters. Is there no end to such wonders?

But the wonders continued and my madness grew. We spent the next five days making our way round the imposing flat top of Auyan Tepui by the Akanan and Carrao rivers – a journey relatively few people have experienced. Our skilled Kamacoto Indian boatmen guided their 20-foot (6 m) dugout motorized canoes through hair-raising rapids and whirlpools, whilst all around, in the virgin forest, brightly coloured birds broke the eerie silence with their strident calls. Sometimes we got out of the canoe and helped push it over water strewn with boulders. Of course, we got drenched and loved it. David Gardiner, the quiet man with a bad shoulder, performed heroically when called upon to swim a tricky section of the river, and Maz gave us an exceptional 'Oh my God', when she encountered veinticuators, the twenty-four-hour ants. We all echoed her sentiments when we set eyes on the miraculous blue morpho butterflies. Oddly enough, they are the only butterflies that I have studied, so I was able to call out their names as they appeared. What a joy to actually see them.

Tiny waterfalls abounded on the banks of the river, their sound amplified and given resonance by the canopy of trees. We saw a 60-foot (18 m) podocarp tree that is related to the pine tree. Its trunk was 4 feet (1.2 m) across, a forest Titan! A dense tangle of giant trees uprooted by mighty winds, whose vast roots had been torn from the soft yielding floor, presented a tricky problem for the Kamaracoto Indians, but unperturbed they solved it without batting an eyelid.

> *And many a knarled trunk was there,*
> *That goes long and stood,*
> *'Til time had wrought them into shapes*
> *Like Pan's fantastic brood*
> *Or still more foul and hideous forms*
> *That pagans carve in wood.*
>
> Thomas Hood, 'The Elm Tree'

For three more days we circumnavigated Auyan Tepui, pushing through the impenetrable rain forest surrounding its base. Its gigantic walls rose up like an iron curtain closing in the whole horizon from north to south. It was at this point in the adventure that I felt a deep yearning to break away from the expedition and explore the rain forest. Auyan Tepui fascinated me and I desperately wanted to climb up to its summit and explore the area where Alexander Laime saw his plesiosaurs while he was searching for diamonds.

> *At first I thought they were great seals, but when I sneaked closer, I saw*
> *they were creatures with enormously long necks and ageless, reptilian*
> *faces. Each had four scale-covered fins instead of legs.*
>
> 'Notes by Alexander Laime in 1955'

The plateau's terrain is totally different from the rocky plateau of Roraima, and most of it is completely unknown. Auyan Tepui is composed of cloud forests, deserts, and rivers. Its geography in fact is not dissimilar to Sir Arthur Conan Doyle's Lost World. I felt so frustrated, and I vowed to return and explore it. As I looked out on those seemingly impenetrable rain forests, I yearned also to explore nearby Aparamen-Tepui and Tukuy-Woki-Yen-Yepuy ('Flower where the hummingbird sucks the nectar'). So much to explore, and so little time to do it in!

As well as being the biggest *tepui*, it is also famed for Angel Falls, leaping from its northern face, and for another twenty waterfalls, all among the highest in the world. Angel Falls are the highest in the world. They were discovered in 1935 by the pilot adventurer, Jimmy Angel who was searching for gold. The falls are a spectacle of extraordinary beauty, as they leap some 3,212 feet (979 m) off the top of the mesa, and plunge straight to the foot of the gorge. The plummeting water vaporises in mid-air forming a glistening white spray which collects in a pool below. This breathtaking cataract is one of the most amazing sights on the American continent. When Jimmy Angel first saw it he said, 'I saw a waterfall that almost made me lose control of my plane.'

When we first saw it from our dugout canoe, we felt the same emotion as Jimmy Angel. It was a phenomenal sight. In the dry season I understand that it is not nearly as impressive, but when we arrived it was in full flood. How my video camera survived the ordeal I will never know, for it was drenched time and time again. In spite of its raging power, we managed to reach its very base. Nick and Anthony actually stood directly beneath it and, miraculously, they somehow managed to stay on their feet.

The following day, above one set of dangerous rapids, the Indians asked everyone to get out of the boat and walk and to join them downstream. After putting on an extra safety-jacket, I was allowed to stay on board so that I could film this section of the river. I quickly forgot the filming and simply held on for dear life as powerful waves swept over the canoe in quick succession. I was convinced that we were about to be pulverized, but the marvellous Indians guided us with great expertise into calmer waters.

It was the final sting in the tale, and a few hours later we were on the banks of the beautiful lagoon of Canaima with picturesque Hacha Falls in the background. The rest of the story, Ladies and Gentlemen, you know.

Throughout the book I have referred quite frequently to Sir Arthur Conan Doyle's great book *The Lost World*. After all, it was the serialization of the book by the BBC in the late 1940s that stirred my imagination. But perversely enough, the moment that Professor Challenger and his companions enter the Lost World it is doomed. The young hero, Edward Malone writes,

> *There are strange red depths in the soul of the most commonplace man. I am tender hearted by nature, and have found my eyes moist many times over the scream of a wounded hare. Yet the bloodlust was on me now. "Shoot into the thick of them! Shoot! Sonny shoot!" cried my companion!*

The companion he was referring to was Lord John Roxton. They were both firing on the 'ape-folk' who lived on the plateau.

'With the massacre of the ape-men,' writes Malone, 'we were in truth masters of the plateau, for the natives looked upon us with a mixture of fear and gratitude.' When the heroes are leaving the plateau, Malone writes:

> *'With much labour we got things up the steps, and then, looking back, took one last long survey of that strange land, soon I fear to be vulgarised, the prey of hunter and prospector, but to each of us a dreamland of glamour and romance.'*

Yes, the Lost World is truly lost when it is found!

I write this because the day before I left Venezuela, I went with Anthony Rivas to the Natural History Museum in Caracas. After an hour or so we entered a half-lit room which had, as its centrepiece, a large model of the Gran Sabana. I was intrigued to see tiny coloured flags all over it. They were the flags of such nations as Japan, Canada, the USA, Britain and Germany. They denoted areas that would be portioned off for each country. To my horror I realized that the flags represented future oil refineries. Apparently, a sea of oil lies under the Gran Sabana. I have been informed that the government of Venezuela is also going to erect electricity pylons straight across the Sabana in the coming year.

What am I to say about this? I don't know. I do know it makes me infinitely sad. Think about it. The Lost World.

Earlier in the book I described that peaceful, idyllic pond the Gam that gave me such happiness in my childhood. It no longer exists. The trees were felled and the pond was filled in, and now a large factory stands on it. With a bit of luck the great crested newts may have found safe havens in the outskirts of the seven fields. As for the Gran Sabana, it looks as though Alexander Laime's plesiosaurs may have company. For if some 'greedy pox-eyed rat bags' have their way then dinosaurs of the nodding metal donkey kind will invade and dip their heads and stick their tongues into the sacred ancient crust of the Lost World. And then Conan Doyle's Lost World will be truly lost, which would be a tragedy. The *tepuis* are two billion years old. They are all different. Each has its own individual ecosystem, because of millions of years of isolation. Each species of plant has adapted to its own particular environment.

I feel that the area around Roraima is in for one hell of a beating, but I'm sure it will survive. The *tepuis* are scattered over an area of some 200,000 square miles (518,000 sq km) of vast impenetrable forests and mighty swirling rivers full of piranha fish and pulsating electric eels. The negative side of man will have a hell of a task conquering this.

Science informs us that a single leaf is riddled with thousands of tiny mouths called 'stomata'. These provide its breathing apparatus.

> *And 'tis my faith that every flower*
> *Enjoys the air it breaths.*
>   William Wordsworth, 'Lines Written in Early Spring'

At one stage in our evolution we used to worship trees. In a great many parts of the world we now decimate them on a vast scale. As I write, Sumatra is once more on fire. The glorious green mountains of South America must be nurtured and protected, they are a large part of the lungs of our beautiful blue world.

You will have gathered by now that I have always been obsessed with dinosaurs. Why? I suppose that when I first heard about them it activated a mysterious part of my race memory. I cannot describe the ecstasy I felt. I virtually trod on air, I walked in light and from that day to this I have never recovered from that sacred experience. To deny my love for dinosaurs, this universe, adventure and our unique planet would be like committing spiritual suicide. As the Bible says, 'I am that I am', and I will kick anybody into the middle of next week if they try to alter me.

In recent years we have become very conscious of our potential to affect the delicate balance of nature. The world that we inhabit has taken at least 4,500 million years to reach its present state. During our short stay on Earth we have subjected it to a great deal of abuse. We now look around in alarm because we realize there is a possibility that the pillaged Earth may not be able to support us much longer. I have always rejoiced in the fact that the dinosaurs were one of the great success stories of evolution, utterly dominating the Earth for over 160 million years. You might say in the Earth's history that they occupied 'the long-stay car park', where we have scarcely entered 'the short-term'.

But could it really be that in some remote corner of the Earth dinosaurs still exist? It delights me to know in this highly technological age, that there are numerous expeditions throughout the world discovering unknown animals. Nature is always full of surprises. In the Gobi Desert, Ivan Mackerle, a scientist and explorer, is searching for the 5-foot (1.5 m) long blood-red Mongolian death worm. It is the stuff of legend. Apparently it lives beneath the shifting sands of the desert, rarely surfacing, and then only to squirt a deadly blast of venom at its predators. Some even believe it has the power to electrocute its victims. At the present time, several expeditions are in the Congo, searching for the frequently seen *Mokele-Mbembe*, an aquatic beast said to resemble an iguanodon. More recently, scientists have discovered a huge kangaroo which lives in trees in Irian Jaya, the western part of New Guinea, and a new species of ox, now named the *Vu Quang* which was discovered on the borders of North Vietnam and Laos. Of course the search still goes on for the Amazonian Bigfoot called *Mapinguari*, which is over 6 feet (1.8 m) tall, with dark red fur, a thunderous roaring voice and a disabling stench. Also in South America, zoologists have discovered a species of peccary, similar to a pig, which was thought to have become extinct millions of years ago. The list is endless. Take the yeti for instance. In North America and Canada it is called Bigfoot or 'Sasquatch', in Russia, the 'Alymas Giant', in China, 'Gigantopithecus' and in Sumatra, 'Orang Pendek'. Reinhold Messner, the great climber and explorer, a stickler for accuracy, claims he has photographs of an adult yeti in Eastern Tibet, feeding its young. He said that it was shy, red-haired and around 6 foot 6 inches (2 m) tall, but he is refusing to release his pictures until he publishes a book in the near future.

In 1974, the Brazilian explorer, Miriano Da Silva had been searching for a settlement of Yatapu Indians on the Brazilian border with Guyana, close to Venezuela, when he encountered a flesh-eating tree. The strange plant released a very distinctive smell that was highly attractive to monkeys and enticed them to climb its trunk. The trees leaves would then totally envelope the unfortunate simians, rendering them inaudible and invisible whilst being digested. A few days later the leaves would unfold and the monkeys' bones would drop to the ground, stripped of flesh. A pretty gruesome tree, ladies and gentlemen, you must admit. The tree is described by the naturalist, Randall Shwartz in his book *Carnivorous Plants*. And what of the Cobra Grande that I mentioned at the beginning of the book? The renowned zoologist, Richard Freeman informs me that reports of its existence pour in daily from Brazil, Columbia and Venezuela. He maintains that there is a good chance that it exists. The reports describe a snake between 50 and 170 feet (15–51 m) long. When I questioned Freeman about this he said:

'The Cobra Grande is also known as *Sucuriju gigante* and *Boiuna* and if it exists it has one huge advantage over the python that may well allow it to attain a greater size. Most pythons are oviparous, that is, they retain eggs inside their bodies until the young hatch, and give birth to them live. But the Cobra Grande is not oviparous and never has to leave the water so its final link with the land is broken. Living in water almost all of the time means that they are buoyed up, and do not have to support their own body weight on land and hence can grow to a very large size. We shall hear a great deal more about the Cobra Grande, I'm sure.'

I do hope that in this epilogue I have not given you the impression that I feel that the world is doomed, far from it!

I do not wish to be a prophet of doom. I think that the good guys will win out in the end, I am absolutely convinced of that. I always keep in mind the image of Pandora. She opened the box and released all those furies. Then, when she realized what she had done, she attempted to close the lid and a little voice said, 'Let me out.' Pandora did so and a tiny creature flew out. Spreading her wet, iridescent wings in the morning light like a blue morpho butterfly, she said: 'I am Hope, I am Hope.'

Ladies and gentlemen, we have hope! There is no doubt at all that the reptilian part of my brain is very active. On our expedition, that handsome fellow Nick Moss said I was a dinosaur. He was right. Therefore I warmly invite you to my underwater kingdom of Otoh Gunga. My love and best wishes to you all.

Brian Blessed, or should I say 'Boss Nass'?

INDEX